Praise for *The Happy Human*

"*At Google it is a high compliment when you call someone 'Googley.' Gopi is one of the most Googley people I know. He says yes to life, creates new opportunities, and is as helpful and inspiring as he is effective in his work. The* Happy Human *is a fun, interesting, and happy way to learn Gopi's insights and experience his ups and downs. A thoroughly good read.*"

— Alan Eagle, Director of Executive Summits, Google; co-author of the *New York Times* bestseller *How Google Works*

"*Being with Gopi makes me happy, and now, even when he is on one of his global adventures, I can get happy reading this book. Teaching with him, I have experienced the insight, kindness, inclusivity, and humility that he brings to the book from his life experiences, which range from village life in India to tech life in Silicon Valley. I often teach a meditation that includes the phrase 'May all beings be happy.' Now Gopi gives us accessible techniques and inspiration to bring that aspiration to life. And you can start right now!*"

— Mirabai Bush, co-founder of the Center for Contemplative Mind in Society; co-developer of Search Inside Yourself, Google; and co-author with Ram Dass of *Walking Each Other Home*

"*In* The Happy Human, *Gopi shows us there isn't an exact formula to follow in order to achieve happiness. Instead, we must simply remember that life is one big experiment— and our only task is to embrace ourselves and the human experience. It is when we do this that we can find true meaning and live a happier, more purpose-filled life.*"

— Cait Flanders, author of *The Year of Less*

"*A good reminder of the important ways we can each change our thinking to have a happier and more meaningful life.*"

— Rabbi Steve Leder, author of *More Beautiful Than Before: How Suffering Transforms Us*

"As a professor in Silicon Valley, I endeavor to give my students skills that will help them innovate in their careers. When Gopi visits my classroom, his effervescent stories remind students of the goal of innovation: to be happy every day, at work and at home, and to help others be happy."

— Ted Ladd, Ph.D., professor of entrepreneurship
at Hult International Business School and
instructor at Harvard University

"Life is a series of waves, of peaks, of ups and downs. No one is happy all the time. But the only thing that really matters in life is being happy. Not just content, not just satisfied, but fulfilled and full of meaning. This is a hard goal to reach, and one that's impossible to live up to all the time. It is too easy to be living well and to not fully appreciate it. . . . In The Happy Human, *Gopi gives you some tips to put into practice to remain fully alive and happy."*

— Amandine Roche, human rights lawyer,
United Nations, and founder
of United Mindful Nations

"As technology races forward at light speed, this is exactly the guide we all desperately need, and we need it now. I will recommend it to my patients, tech clients, and everyone in my community, since there's not a single person who cannot benefit from Gopi's book."

— Ronesh Sinha, M.D., physician, speaker, and
author of *The South Asian Health Solution*

"I connected profoundly with The Happy Human, *especially how life's sorrows are part of the whole human experience and how these can and do ultimately lead to happiness. . . . Gopi is a gifted storyteller whose delivery is a mixture of wisdom, humor, and compassion.* The Happy Human *is sure to inspire your heart and intellect."*

— Karen Guggenheim, CEO of WOHASU and
co-founder of the World Happiness Summit

THE
HAPPY
HUMAN

ALSO BY GOPI KALLAYIL

*The Internet to the Inner-Net: Five Ways to Reset
Your Connection and Live a Conscious Life*

The above is available at your local bookstore,
or may be ordered by visiting:

Hay House USA: www.hayhouse.com®
Hay House Australia: www.hayhouse.com.au
Hay House UK: www.hayhouse.co.uk
Hay House India: www.hayhouse.co.in

***

THE
HAPPY
HUMAN

Being Real *in an* Artificially
Intelligent World

GPI
KALLAYIL

HAY
HOUSE

HAY HOUSE, INC.
Carlsbad, California • New York City
London • Sydney • New Delhi

Library of Congress has cataloged the earlier edition as follows:

Names: Kallayil , Gopi, author.
Title: The happy human : getting real in an artificially intelligent world /
    Gopi Kallayil.
Description: Carlsbad, California : Hay House, [2018]
Identifiers: LCCN 2018016400 | ISBN 9781401946227 (hardcover : alk.
paper)
Subjects: LCSH: Conduct of life. | Happiness. | Self-realization. | Kallayil
, Gopi--Philosophy.
Classification: LCC BJ1589 .K353 2018 | DDC 158--dc23 LC record avail-
able at https://lccn.loc.gov/2018016400

Tradepaper ISBN: 978-1-4019-4623-4
E-book ISBN: 978-1-4019-5412-3

1st edition, September 2018
2nd edition, July 2020

Printed in the United States of America

To my father and mother
for giving me life and happiness.

To my Gurus
Rama Devi, Tara Devi, Amma
for teaching me to look for happiness
within.

C☺NTENTS

F☺REWORD

I met Gopi at the first World Happiness Summit in 2017, where I spoke about the Science of Happiness and he spoke about the Internet to the Inner-Net. We also spoke about this book, which he was just starting to write, and worried about a bit. When he gave me the book to read, I was struck by the profound simplicity of his writing. On the one hand, I could certainly relate to the ideas he wrote about, and yet on the other hand reading the book deepened my understanding—and my experience—of the Happy Human.

Those writing about the pursuit of happiness are often criticized for being detached idealists. There is so much pain in the world, levels of depression and anxiety are on the rise, and you're concerned with happiness? Surely dealing with the dominance of the Suffering Human should precede dealing with the rare or absent phenomenon of the Happy Human. A second, related criticism aimed at those who explore and thus promote the pursuit of happiness is that they are spreading selfishness. How can you write about happiness while there is so much misery in the world? How can you encourage people to spend time on their personal flourishing when millions across our global village are hungry? Shouldn't we direct our personal pursuit and our collective concern toward studying and alleviating suffering and injustice? The two classes of criticism—concerning the detached and selfish nature of the pursuit of happiness—are valuable in that they can help us more fully understand what happiness is and is not, and why in fact exploring the concept of the Happy Human is so important for us, personally and collectively.

I'll begin by looking at the first criticism, that of happiness being a detached pursuit that does not take into consideration human suffering. Throughout this book Gopi points out that leading a full life is about embracing failures and hardships and disappointments. He generously, unselfconsciously, and often hilariously tells of his own run-ins with the more challenging aspects of humanity, noting that they're just as important to living a full life as celebrating success and freedom and purpose. The Happy Human Gopi and I both write of is not reflected in an indifferent smiley face or in the detached call to not worry and be happy. A Happy Human is not in conflict with her humanity, giving herself the permission to be human. This permission is crucial. Gopi suggests we surround ourselves with people who applaud our being our true selves—human beings—and offers insights and examples from his life in Silicon Valley and at Google, where risk taking is encouraged and failure is seen as a door to new possibilities, new problems, new solutions. We can scale these examples to our everyday lives.

The idea of the permission to be human has become central to my personal pursuit of a happier life as well as to my teaching on happiness. I initially thought of this idea during the first year when I taught positive psychology at Harvard. I was having a meal in Leverett House, one of Harvard's undergraduate dining halls, when Matt, an undergraduate I had met previously, joined me. He told me that he'd heard that I was teaching a class on happiness, and that his roommate was in it. He let me know that he might take the class next year if it did not conflict with other classes he needed to take to graduate. And then he said: "But you know, Tal, now that you are teaching this class, you've got to be careful." I didn't get it. He continued: "Tal, you've got to watch out." I asked him why I needed to be careful and watch out. He said, "Because if I see you unhappy I'll tell my roommate." Matt smiled, as did I. He was clearly joking, or at least half joking. The assumption underlying his comment, though, was a serious and pervasive one—namely, that the ultimate goal of pursuing happiness is a life devoid of unhappiness, and that a person teaching a class on happiness should surely be exempt from any and all unpleasant emotions.

This assumption is detached, unrealistic. There are only two kinds of people who do not experience painful emotions, such as disappointment, sadness, anxiety, envy, or anger. The first kind of people who are largely exempt from painful emotions are the psychopaths. The second kind are . . . dead. The Happy Human, the ideal that Gopi and others uphold and pursue, is neither a psychopath nor is he dead—he cares deeply, sheds tears of compassion and sadness. The Happy Human is anything but detached—he is neither detached from his own suffering nor from the suffering of others. At the same time, he is not detached from his own and others' potential for joy and pleasure and delight. He embraces his full humanity, giving himself the permission to be fully human. And in doing so, as Gopi notes—citing Silicon Valley's culture of radical innovation and Burning Man's policy of radical inclusion—we invite others to do the same. Moreover, the Happy Human, neither being a psychopath nor dead, worries about the state of the world and acts toward alleviating suffering—her own as well as others'. And this is why describing her as selfish, or as *merely* selfish, which is the implication of the second criticism I outlined above, fails to capture the Happy Human's full nature.

For centuries, philosophers and linguists created a clear and unbridgeable schism between selfishness and selflessness, between egoism and altruism. While a person described as an egoist, as selfish, is considered unkind, immoral, and even evil, an altruistic and selfless person is kind, moral, and noble. The negative connotations associated with selfishness stem primarily from Western religion and philosophy. Immanuel Kant, for instance, arguably the most influential philosopher of the modern era, tells us that for an act to have moral worth, it must be undertaken out of a sense of duty. When we act selfishly, then, we preclude the possibility of our action being a moral one. According to Kant, if a person helps another because he feels inclined to do so—because it makes him feel good—what he does has no moral value.

The division between the selfish and the selfless does not stand the test of reality. Bridging the gap between the two seeming opposites—between egoism and altruism, between concern for oneself and concern for others—is none other than our nature. We are so constituted that we care about other people, and consequently that we enjoy helping them. In fact, contributing to other people's welfare is one of the most powerful sources of happiness in life. More and more research is showing that we derive a great deal of personal benefit by being generous and kind. For example, a study conducted by Harvard Business School and the University of British Columbia showed that those who were given money and gave it to others enjoyed a larger increase in their levels of happiness than those who spent the same amount of money on themselves. Other research by UC–Riverside psychologist Sonja Lyubomirsky demonstrates that acting kindly toward others is one of the best ways to increase one's own happiness.

A generous act, therefore, can be perceived as altruistic—if by altruistic we mean helping others—as well as egoistic—if by egoistic we mean helping ourselves. If, on the other hand, we see egoism and altruism as antonyms, as irreconcilable opposites, then a generous act can be neither.

The relationship between helping others (being generous) and helping ourselves (feeling better) is not restricted to the former contributing to the latter. The relationship works in the opposite direction as well: when we help ourselves feel better, we are more likely to be generous toward others. Research by Alice Isen and her colleagues shows that when people are made to feel good—even by trivial means such as receiving a cookie or finding a dime in a phone booth—they are more likely to help others. Barbara Fredrickson demonstrated that the experience of positive emotions broadens our perspective so that we see beyond our narrow self-interest, and also helps us build healthy relationships.

What we end up with is a self-reinforcing loop between helping others and helping our self—in that the more generous we are (the more we help others), the happier we become (the more we help our self); the happier we become, the more likely we are to be generous, and so on.

HELPING OTHERS

HELPING SELF

This "upward spiral of generosity" which relies on the natural interrelationship between self and others clearly demonstrates that the egoism-altruism divide is unfounded. When I help myself by pursuing happiness, my capacity for generosity is significantly amplified—the benefit to others is real. At the same time, when I help others, I am, also, being selfish—the benefit to my personal happiness is real. In fact, there is so much benefit to the person who contributes to others that I often think that there is no more selfish act than a generous act.

Equating selflessness and altruism (and by extension unhappiness) with morality while associating selfishness and egoism (and by extension happiness) with immorality, can lead to unhealthy, sometimes disastrous, outcome. On the macro, national level we can see the real-life consequences of governments that advocated altruism and tried to eradicate selfishness. Communist Russia and Nazi Germany are but two examples of regimes that waged war against our selfish nature, sacrificing individual wants and inclinations for the sake of the Collective or State. These regimes established their power by attacking the Happy Human as selfish (which is partially true) and therefore as immoral (which is patently false). By the time subjects of these governments understood the bloody consequences of waging war with our selfish nature—the part of our nature that aspires to and pursues personal happiness—millions of lives had already been ruined.

On an individual level, the idea that pursuing personal happiness is selfish and therefore bad inflicts unnecessary emotional pain and undermines our innate desire to help others. Given that Kant's idea of what constitutes a moral act is so deeply rooted in our cultural ethos—to the point that it is treated as an axiom—when people do good and feel good about it, they are fast to dismiss their act as unworthy. Instead of the upward spiral of generosity described above—where a generous act would lead to positive emotions that would then lead to more generous acts, more positive emotions, and so on—the spiral is blocked as soon as we feel good about helping others. We may feel guilt over feeling good and being selfish, or generally unworthy for not being able to carry out a moral act. Given the ambivalence and confusion generated by the help we provide others, we are less likely to help others again and put ourselves in this situation in the future.

There are very few things in life that can potentially provide as much happiness as helping other people. Gopi also stresses this point. Rather than fighting our innate constitution, we should revel in this wonderful part of our nature. It is then that every act of generosity further strengthens our desire to do more good for more people.

The generous person does not negate the self (i.e., selfless), nor is he acting in opposition to his egoistic nature (i.e., altruistically). It is therefore that I suggest a different, more appropriate word that encompasses within it the goodness of well-intentioned proponents of selfishness and selflessness: selfulness. A selful person cares about herself and at the same time about others, is generous toward herself and toward others.

In other languages, there are precedents to a word that encompasses both. For example, the word *tsewa* is Tibetan for compassion and caring, and it refers equally to self and others. In the words of the Dalai Lama, whom Gopi had the privilege of meeting, "Compassion, or *tsewa*, as it is understood in the Tibetan tradition, is a state of mind or way of being where you extend how you relate to yourself toward others as well." Not only does the Tibetan understanding of compassion not negate self-love; it elevates it as the primary form of love, a precondition for the love of others:

> Yourself first, and then in a more advanced way the aspiration will embrace others. In a way, high levels of compassion are nothing but an advanced state of that self-interest. That's why it is hard for people who have a strong sense of self-hatred to have genuine compassion toward others. There is no anchor, no basis to start from.

The Dalai Lama is essentially describing how starting with self-love does not only lead to happier individuals, it leads to happier relationships—and by extension, a happier society.

The reciprocal relationship between giving and receiving, between taking care of others and taking care of oneself, is also captured in the ancient language of the Bible. In Hebrew, the word for giving comes from the root NATAN, which is a palindrome—meaning, it is symmetrical and can be read from left to right or right to left. This suggests that when we give, we are given back, we receive, and when we receive, we also give.

The Happy Human that Gopi presents us as his ideal is a person who lives life fully—embracing any and all emotions. A Happy Human is a selful person, a compassionate, generous individual. And it is by striving toward the ideal that Gopi brilliantly and humbly delineates in the following pages that we can fulfill our personal potential for happiness, and our society's potential for humaneness.

Tal Ben-Shahar, Ph.D.
May 2018

Tal Ben-Shahar, an author and lecturer, taught two of the largest classes in Harvard University's history: Positive Psychology and The Psychology of Leadership. Today, Tal consults and lectures around the world to executives in multinational corporations, the general public, and at-risk populations. Topics include leadership, happiness, education, innovation, ethics, self-esteem, resilience, goal setting, and mindfulness. His books, including Happier *and* Choose the Life You Want, *have been translated into more than 25 languages and have appeared on bestseller lists around the world.*

HAPPINESS IS
A CH☺ICE

The purpose of our lives is to be happy.
— THE 14TH DALAI LAMA

Every quarter or so, corporate America and companies around the world hold performance evaluations, a process that's very subjective, and because of that, inherently flawed. It's a period of angst. Before the evaluations, people worry about how they'll do. After, they may go through a period of suffering because they were told they didn't do well, or because they did well but not as well as they'd hoped. There's always that cognitive dissonance and perception gap between how we perceive our accomplishments and how others perceive them. Other people might be unhappy because they didn't get promoted, or they were promoted but the promotion wasn't to the position they wanted, or it was too long coming. There's a lot of stress around titles and advancement. I'm not immune.

A few years ago, just after our quarterly reviews at Google, I was walking in the early morning with my good friend and mentor, Stuart Newton, planning to discuss my own angst. Once a month, Stuart schedules a 7 A.M. chat with me to touch base. We grab a cup of chai from the cafeteria and walk along the path winding through the green, sometimes brown, rolling hills of Shoreline Park across from the Google campus. These walks are my chance to ask for advice and guidance and talk about what's on my mind, personally and professionally, which can often be about setting goals, staying focused, managing my time, the sorry state of my social life.

That morning, I was in a good mood, for the most part. I'd recently returned from Dharamsala, where I'd met His Holiness the Dalai Lama. That meeting was number 36 on my list of 100 things I wanted to do with my life. Soon after I wrote the list, through steps I took, serendipity, and possibly good fortune, I had the opportunity to wait with a group of Americans for an audience with the Dalai Lama. When I'd hesitated about traveling 12,000 miles with no guarantee I'd be able to meet with His Holiness in private, Stuart had nudged me: "You asked the universe, and it has opened a door. Now you must walk through it." Two weeks later, I sat in a small propeller plane, peering down at the tiny Kangra Airport in the Himalayas, where, after we landed, Lama Phuntso, the Dalai Lama's personal tailor (even a monk's russet robes have their own society of elegant tailors, I suppose) whisked me away into a mystical Shangri La–like environment.

As we walked, I told Stuart about the trip, how happy I was, and how well everything was going in my personal life. I expressed some consternation about career growth, promotion cycles, aspirations, and titles, my title—all those imprisoning mental constructs we create for ourselves in the working world.

Stuart held up his hand. "Gopi, wait. Stop, stop, stop. Let's look at this from a different angle. Let me ask you, what title would you want the Dalai Lama to give you?"

I thought for a moment. His Holiness is a man who's been stripped of everything. He's the spiritual leader of

Tibet, but that country was taken away from him. He's in his 80s now and has been living in exile since he was 14 years old. Because he can't go back to his land, he's had to perform sacred ceremonies in other parts of the world—Barcelona; Sydney; Bloomington, Indiana—all miles from his home and his people. The Dalai Lama doesn't even possess a passport. Instead, he has a refugee certificate. Yet there's a level of joy and mirth that you can perceive when you interact with him. He laughs from deep within his belly. Such a sense of joy and happiness. You get caught up in it.

Thinking of that joy, I answered Stuart. "The Happy Human," I said. "That's the title I'd want the Dalai Lama to give to me."

"Gopi, let me tell you this," Stuart said. "If you're truly a happy human, and that's the title you would want the Dalai Lama to give to you, then that title is higher than senior vice president, because the senior vice president also wants to be happy but could actually be pretty miserable behind the stoic exterior. By the time many people achieve their coveted titles, they just want more than anything else to be happy. But they struggle. They still feel angst. The achievement can feel empty. They may have spent forty years climbing a certain ladder, only to get to the top and discover that the ladder was leaning against the wrong wall."

Immediately I felt lighter and, as always, grateful that Stuart is my mentor, and in that moment, I decided to make "Happy Human" an important value and identity for myself. A few days later, I had new personal cards made. One side shows a picture of me smiling, full of happiness. The other side reads "Happy Human." Now, when I meet people socially—at the Wharton Entrepreneurship dinner, an Electric Sheep party at The Battery, a Burning Man cultural collaborators' gathering, the Wisdom 2.0 speakers' dinner, the Yoga Festival, and the ad:tech conference evening event—I hand out that card. It immediately triggers an interesting conversation and shifts perceptions—mine and the person's I've handed the card to. As Jack Kornfield says in *Buddha's Little Instruction Book*, "In the end, these things matter most: How well did you love? How fully did you live? How deeply did you let go?"

When I think about fully living life, these questions come to mind: Are you hopeful? Are you contributing? Are you living the life you want? Are you making a difference? Are you pursuing what's important to you, what aligns with what you value most? I decided long ago that the three things I value most are peace of mind, freedom, and happiness. I believe these values are held dear by all human beings. They're intertwined. The key to my happiness comes from embracing the "human" in "Happy Human." It's not just about being happy, it's about being human. For me, that means being completely true to who I am, to what matters to me. If that means leaving my native country to seek uncertain employment in an unfamiliar country because seeing the world had long been a dream of mine, then so be it. If that means quitting a lucrative job that would shoot me ahead on my career path because I realize the work isn't resonating with me, sign me up. And if that means facing almost certain rejection by requesting an audience with the Dalai Lama because it's on my bucket list and what do I have to lose by trying, then that's what I'll do.

When we're true to who we are, when we revel in and express our authentic selves, embrace our human flaws, feel compassion for ourselves and one another as we make our way in life, we can discover enormous inner freedom, even if circumstances prevent us from external freedom. We can feel peace. Joy. We can feel happy.

I attribute much of my happiness to a combination of the wisdom practices I learned growing up in India and the fulfillment I've found working in the tech industry, providing billions of people with access to information and tools that otherwise were previously unavailable to them. I often tell people I feel lucky to have won the ovarian lottery, meaning I feel incredibly blessed to have been born into a culture where practicing yoga and meditation have been a part of people's daily lives for hundreds of years. My yoga and meditation practices help me tap into and foster a deep sense of joy. They also help provide me with the confidence to embrace the human experience fully—going for it, full-out, even if, maybe especially if, I fall on my face. And I have. Many times. I sang live at Burning Man, even though I sing slightly off-key. I was terrified. I entered a triathlon, which involved swimming in a lake. Before that, I'd only swum in a pool, always within four feet of an edge to grab on to. I nearly drowned. I spoke at Toastmasters, just a few months after arriving from South Asia with no job and $7,000 to my name. I was awful. But I learned. I kept going. I got better.

Without failure, I wouldn't have had the successes I've had, both in my personal life and in my professional career. I wouldn't feel the sense of freedom and joy. Working in Silicon Valley has helped me take risks, because tech companies encourage failing, and failing big. One of the keys to Google's success is their willingness to fail. And we fail most of the time. But because we fail so much and so often, we learn a lot, experience a lot, and we then become successful. It's fascinating that an industry that's all about the artificial—electronic brains, social media personas, driverless cars, fake store greeters who offer us movies and books the minute we log on to Netflix or Amazon—also embraces human fallibility more than almost any other industry.

How do we fully embrace ourselves and the human experience? How do we find the confidence to risk, fall on our faces, get back up again, and live expansive lives? What are the internal shifts we can make that will get us to this place of joy? In this book, I'll share my own journey, the risks and experiments that have worked (and fabulously failed) along the way. I'll talk about some of the thinking of the tech industry that sparks innovation and encourages mistakes, thinking we can adapt for our own personal and professional lives. What Jon Kabat-Zinn refers to as "full catastrophe living," leaning into the full catastrophe of everything life throws at you. And the ability to put the bumps in the road in perspective.

You'll also read about other people's journeys. People I've met in my travels, through projects for Google, and while researching this book. People such as Sunita Danuwar, founder of Shakti Samuha, an organization dedicated to working against sex trafficking, and Nicole Thakuri-Wick, who founded NAG, Home of New Hopes, an institution that provides a home—shelter, education, and medical care—for kids who were living on the street. These women took huge risks, dug deep for inner resources, and found peace, freedom, meaning, and happiness within, despite extremely challenging circumstances. These are people who live their lives from a place of being 100 percent true to who they are, and they are helping others do the same.

The book is divided into three parts that I feel are the progressive pieces to the happiness puzzle: (1) finding meaning and purpose, (2) rewriting your own stories, and finally, (3) living your life to the max, happy in your own skin, with no apologies—and, when you get to this third part, surrounding yourself with a community of supportive people and sharing your purpose, joy, and bumbling, fallible, free, 100 percent humanness with them. When you share yourself in this way with others who are doing the same, you can shift the world. I'll go into more detail in the next chapters.

As you read through the book, you move from self-discovery to resilience to grabbing life by the tail, totally happy with who you are. Each chapter explores a different part of the happiness equation—becoming your own best friend; expecting miracles; singing in public, loud and unashamedly off-key because it's a dream of yours, because it makes you happy.

There's been an enormous amount of research on happiness in the corporate world, the spiritual world, and political spheres. How do you get it? What are the benefits? How do you measure it? In a book review of *Happier?* and *The Hope Circuit* in *The Wall Street Journal*, Carol Travis wrote, "The elusive nature of happiness may be the reason our Founding Fathers promised us its pursuit and not its capture. Yet the failure to nab it in our physiological nets is a major reason the happiness-pursuit industry has thrived for centuries. If people maintain wrongheaded definitions and expectations of happiness, after all, they won't know it when it curls up on their laps asking to be petted. And if people can't know happiness, even when they feel it, the market for helping them do so will keep growing. This being America, it has."

It's my hypothesis that no matter how much research we've conducted, how much life has changed, how much we've evolved as human beings, the levels of happiness and unhappiness are still about the same as they were 100 years ago, 1,000 years ago, and long before that. I have no way of proving this, because we haven't been benchmarking happiness, but I believe the conditions for happiness are available to us. They're known to us. Yet each one of us has to go through the cycle of learning these conditions and adopting them. I heard Krishna Das speak at the Sivananda Ashram in the Bahamas about finding our own path to happiness and walking that path. "No one else can do it for us," he said. To achieve this state of happiness, we have to rework and retool ourselves. This was true thousands of years ago. It's true now. And it will be true 10 years, 50 years, 100 years from now. As author and Buddhist meditation teacher Sharon Salzberg says, "Happiness is not a feeling. It's an ability we can learn and cultivate." It's my hope that this book can help accelerate this process slightly for you.

PART I

FIND MEANING AND PURP☺SE

Studies show that people who are happiest, most resilient, and unapologetic about embracing life have found a deep sense of purpose, one that resonates, that lights them up, and in turn lights up others. How do you find that purpose? You sit, listen, observe. You pause. "Pausing," writes Rachel O'Meara, "offers you a chance to remember what 'lights you up.'" And deep down, you know what that is. It doesn't matter if you pause for two weeks, two days, or even two minutes. The point is, you need to be by yourself. Pausing is really creating a little bit of spaciousness inside, and in that pause, that space, you reconnect with yourself. Monks Mingyur Rinpoche and Matthieu Ricard paused for years in a cave. Bill Gates pauses for two weeks a year. Do what works for you. Take time off from your job, your life, your kids. Pause for a minute. Pause for a weekend. Or you can do as Thoreau did and set up camp in a small cabin in the woods and pause for two years, two months, and two days. Whatever it takes.

MUDDLING INT☺ HAPPINESS

In every moment, the universe is whispering to you. . . . [Y]ou are surrounded by personal messages from the world around you.
— DENISE LINN, *THE SECRET LANGUAGE OF SIGNS*

Toward the end of 2016, while I was traveling through southern India, I went through my annual process of setting goals for the next year. For the most part, I was happily looking forward to the new year, but at the same time, I was feeling a bit unhappy, intimidated, and apprehensive about one of the biggest projects in front of me in 2017—writing this book. Somehow I'd managed to finish my first book, *The Internet to the Inner-Net*, and while completing that book should have given me the confidence to write this one, it didn't. In fact, this time the stress was worse, because for my first book, I had the context for writing about balancing the outer technologies with the inner technologies—our brain, our body, our breath, our consciousness. But happiness? That was a whole new game. Sure, I'm happy, and my personal card bears the title "Happy Human," but where would I find the inspiration, material, wisdom to write a book about happiness?

3

Throughout my time in India, I felt miserable, ruminating on happiness. While standing in Tadasana (Mountain Pose) at sunrise at the spiritual center in Mangalore, I worried. At the India Yoga Festival, while lounging on the deck of a typical Kerala houseboat, sipping masala chai under a thatched palm roof, my anxiety crept in. At my parents' home in Thrissur, Kerala, where I was supposed to be relaxing, I felt anything but relaxed.

The weather at my parents' house was amazing—sunny, balmy, the leaves on the coconut trees and banana trees rustling in the breeze. But was I outside on the patio (or even looking out the window) or spending time with my parents? No. Every spare moment I had, I was upstairs in the low-ceilinged home office on my computer, checking on work and speaking engagements, staying connected to my e-mail, putting myself in a spatial orbit of the United States. My body was in India, but my mind and attention were 10,000 miles away.

This preoccupation occurs every time I visit. But it was worse than usual, because when I wasn't taking care of something to do with Google, I was working on this book. My three siblings, always horrified about how I can spend my time upstairs when I should be spending time with my parents, were more aghast than they normally are. "Why did you buy a ticket and fly all the way just to transport your physical body but not your attention and your spirit?" my sisters asked.

When I visit, my mom often asks me, in Malayalam, the language spoken in my home state of Kerala, "What's the point in coming here? You're sitting there going tap tap tap on that thing." It's got to be annoying. I'm sure all they hear downstairs is clickety clack. Clack, clack, clack, backspace, backspace, backspace, kaboom, return.

This time, my mom was so distressed, she called my brother in the United States, who first wrote a strongly worded e-mail, then called immediately to scold me. There was my brother, four years younger than I am, calling all the way from Portland, Oregon, saying, "Go downstairs. Get away from the computer. Spend some time with Mom and Dad." So, duly chastised, I went downstairs. But no wonder I felt so unhappy and tense, right? No wonder we all did.

THE QUEST FOR HAPPINESS

Happiness is one of the most universal of values, virtues, and pursuits. It doesn't matter which country or what species. As the Dalai Lama says, "Like oneself, all other sentient beings are equal in having this wish to be happy and to overcome suffering." The dog wants to be happy, the cat, the lion, the elephant. Every sentient being—we all want it. It doesn't matter what age. From a little baby to an older adult, from the members of the scavenger caste in India, whom Gandhi called the *harijan*, the people of God, to, as of this writing, the president of the United States tweeting at 4 A.M.—all want happiness. It's one of everyone's favorite topics. And thanks to the American marketing machine, there's an entire industry around it. It's huge. You can google "books on happiness in English." I did. Nearly 45 million results. "Happiness conferences," 4 million results. "Happiness trainings," 499,000. On Amazon, I searched "happiness books" and got 137,563. "Happiness magazines," 873.

Yet with all this focus on happiness, we have no clear consensus about what exactly defines or drives that feeling so fundamental to the human condition. Why, after a million years of evolution, we still haven't nailed what happiness is, what drives our need for it, and how we get there. Other fundamentals we know more about—what drives hunger and how to satisfy our body's needs with a nutritious meal; what drives the need for sleep and how to restore ourselves by lying down, closing our eyes, and logging a good eight hours. Why we crave human connection, which the fabric of our society supports. But when it comes to happiness, it's not quite clear, which is why I was feeling a bit of angst about the topic.

But then, finally—and more than once during my trip—I took a breath, paused, and reminded myself that in these moments of confusion, worry, and doubt, sometimes you just have to trust that things will start coming together. That trust can lead to happiness.

THE SYNCHRONOUS UNIVERSE

There's a generally held belief that when some topic or project is important to you, suddenly everything around you reflects that topic. People show up. Books materialize to guide you. Opportunities appear seemingly out of nowhere. Once I trusted, that's what happened—things magically, miraculously started showing up to support my writing this book. My friend Stuart Newton presented me with a one-year subscription to a magazine called *Live Happy*—six issues of a publication devoted to just that. Then I discovered Silvia Garcia, former global director of the Happiness Institute at Coca-Cola, whose job was to help the company cultivate happiness. She runs her own company now, Feel Logic, and is a speaker about the learnings of happiness. When I met her, she told me about the inaugural World Happiness Summit, where experts were going to speak about the subject.

When you trust that the universe will provide resources, and then things start showing up, you want to pay attention and follow the bread crumbs. So I contacted the World Happiness Summit in Miami and was invited to be the keynote speaker along with Mo Gawdat, my esteemed colleague at Google and the author of *Solve for Happy: Engineer Your Path to Joy*, in which he proposes an algorithm based on an understanding of how the brain takes in and processes joy and sadness. I was also invited to meet with a team led by the Minister of State for Happiness from the United Arab Emirates, Ohood Al Roumi, one of 8 female ministers in the 29-member Cabinet of the UAE.

Then I was looking through a stack of magazines in my office at home and came across an old copy of *The Economist* from 2006. The cover story was "Happiness (and How to Measure It)." The article was written in the tone of economists—cautious, a bit grim—and even though the entire article is about happiness, it's pretty dismal. The last line of the editorial reads, "Capitalism can make you well off. It also leaves you free to be as unhappy as you choose." But more about that subject later.

Finally, an e-mail showed up in my in-box announcing a class called Solving for Happy. Normally, with the filter I have, large general announcements like that go into a separate folder that I rarely look through. It's too much volume to handle. But I was searching through my in-box for I'm not sure what now, and it showed up. The class was to be conducted by one of my most respected colleagues, the aforementioned Mo Gawdat, chief business officer for Google X. This is a semi-secret lab whose mission is "to invent and launch 'moonshot' technologies that we hope could someday make the world a radically better place." Google defines *moonshot* as "a project or proposal that addresses a huge problem, proposes a radical solution, and uses breakthrough technology to get there. Moonshot projects include Google Glass, Google Brain (artificial intelligence and machine learning, which is the ability to learn from new data, without programming), and Waymo (Google's self-driving car project). Mo has brought the type of thinking employed at X to the topic of happiness. *Wow.* I signed up immediately. Now there's a long waiting list. Had I waited, I never would have gotten into the class.

So there I was, back at home in California, surrounded by access to all these opportunities and resources that had suddenly shown up out of nowhere. I was wired for happiness, my antennae were up—all because of this book I needed to write. At that point, I felt somewhat confident that I could write about this topic with a degree of authority, because in addition to these resources, for the most part I'm a genuinely happy person. People often comment on it, so I'm not totally deluding myself.

But I will say that any answers I've found, I've learned by risking, stumbling, making false starts, taking wrong turns, figuring things out on the fly. Or not. Playing the fool, falling on my face. I don't care. Because I always learn. I always grow. That's what I want for you: to benefit from all I've learned, to try out the inspiration and tips on these pages, and to bump into your own walls, knowing that exploring the inner world, pausing, listening—all of which we'll explore in these pages—will make the journey so much easier. You'll find a deep trust in yourself, happiness in who you are. You'll be there for yourself, cheering yourself on, listening to your inner guidance, and then, when you leap, you'll land softly. On your feet.

WHAT IS
IN THE
HAPPINESS
MASALA?

If you want others to be happy,
practice compassion. If you want to be
happy, practice compassion.
— THE 14TH DALAI LAMA

Sylvia Garcia of the Happiness Institute has spent more than a decade involved in the discoveries of science and happiness. Drawing from neuroscience and ancient wisdom traditions, she defines happiness as "an estate of your mind and spirit that's opposite to hopelessness. Following this definition," she says, "you find happy people actively helping things get better, actively cultivating their mind, body, and spirit with the purpose of creating a greater good for all." What is her critical ingredient for happiness? "Loving yourself and others kindly, which allows nourishing real and intimate relationships."

Happiness takes commitment, action, love.

As a teenager, I suppose I was what you'd call happy, but I still suffered the classic hormone-fueled angst and confusion, caught in that blur between childhood and adulthood, searching for something, though I had no idea what. As is typical, I felt unaccountably sad at times. I was far too preoccupied with myself, sometimes angry at anything and everything. When you're in an unhappy state, and particularly at that point in life, the teen years, you're often aware of only one movie, and that's *your* movie. You're the hero in that movie, the lead actor, and you have no idea about what else is out there. At that age, you don't have the sophistication to look at research showing that teenagers all over the world are miserable or unhappy. You just know you're feeling somewhat miserable that day.

Looking back, and having read a lot of research and done a lot of work on myself, I know now much of my dissatisfaction and unhappiness had to do with not living in the present. My ruminations on the past and my brooding about the future coupled with my lack of confidence and insecurity led to that level of unhappiness. Then there was the business of peer pressure, the constant comparison. That's a game you're destined to lose.

Now I can confidently say I've broken out of a lot of that over the years, and it's been an interesting and fun journey. Journeying toward happiness was itself cause for happiness. And while some research indicates that pursuing happiness is a recipe for unhappiness, that wasn't the case for me. Maybe that's because of the pieces involved, the three key elements I mentioned earlier that I believe are crucial for happiness:

1. Finding purpose in our lives, which gives us meaning and direction

2. Reframing the stories we tell ourselves that make us unhappy or imprison us, which will empower us

3. Being comfortable in our own skin, absolutely 100 percent true to and happy with who we are, which will enable us to go forth and live a full life, without apology, spreading our purpose and our 100 percent fallible, fully human, joyous self with others

Looking at the first point, it's critical to feel that what we're doing is worth doing, that our life is worth living. According to data from the Centers for Disease Control and Prevention, four out of ten Americans have not discovered a satisfying life purpose, which is essential to a feeling of well-being that's crucial to happiness. In fact, while animals and humans both wish for happiness, as human beings our search for meaning sets us apart.

FIND YOUR MEANING AND PURPOSE

Even as a somewhat anxious, angst-ridden adolescent, I realized early on that there were areas I was fiercely drawn to that eventually led me to a greater purpose. I had a great love for physics and electronics and wanted to pursue an education in engineering and technology. In high school and college, I was focused on building my skills in debate, public speaking, elocution, and leadership. I wanted to explore the horizons of a life beyond the confines of my home, and finally, I was quite drawn to exploring the inner life through yoga and meditation, from which I derived an incredible sense of joy.

Over time, I arrived at my own meaning and purpose in life, which is to live to my highest potential and to help others realize their own. My meaning and purpose stem from a place of deep joy. My work at Google aligns with my meaning and purpose. I'm doing work I deeply believe in—helping to level the playing field for humanity by providing access to information people might not otherwise be able to get their hands on. In an age in which information powers the world, being a part of helping others to reach their potential brings me a great sense of meaning and purpose.

Mo Gawdat found a new purpose when his 21-year-old son, Ali, died during routine surgery. In *Solve for Happy*, he writes about how he arrived at a point where, rather than grieving as he dealt with what is considered one of the most stressful things for anyone human, he decided to honor and celebrate his son's life. He would bring new meaning to his own life by employing everything he'd learned from his son about happiness, combined with his own theories, to make 10 million people happier. His moonshot for his son? To create "a small-scale, global pandemic of Ali-style joy." That's a profound sense of mission and purpose for any human being.

CHANGE YOUR STORY

Mo's story illustrates my second point—the importance of reframing events and retelling the story in your head because at the end of the day, happiness is actually driven not by events but by your interpretation of them. As Stoic philosopher Epictetus said 2,000 years ago, "Men are disturbed not by things, but by the views which they take of things." I've been blessed to meet people around the world who've survived horrendous experiences, reframed their stories, and gone on to live deeply meaningful lives. You'll read some of their stories in this book.

LIVE WITH AUTHENTICITY

I believe you become a lot happier the day you start living your own life, in your own body, in your own movie.

And letting your own story unfold as opposed to someone else's life and someone else's expectations and someone else's mood. Just be yourself and live the life that you want to live and are meant to live, which sets you on a path to inner freedom and happiness. That takes courage.

As I sat in Mo Gawdat's Solving for Happy class, I was struck by his courage. Here's a very busy senior business executive who just walked away from it all for six months to work on his mission of spreading happiness. There's something very affirming about someone at that level who spends so much time thinking about happiness and takes a six-month sabbatical to teach it to others. While he was on sabbatical, he had no title, because he wasn't playing the role of the chief. He was just a Googler on leave. He had no staff reporting to him, no personal assistant to manage his time. He chose that. That's an act of courage to say, "This is so important to me, I'm going to take six months off to talk about what I went through so people can take lessons from that and be happy." There's something very empowering and refreshing about that.

When you've got these three ingredients down, it's so much easier to take risks, to make a difference in the world, or, as Steve Jobs said, "Make a dent in the universe."

TAKE RISKS

Growing up, I didn't take many risks. My family was fairly risk-averse. They'd been rice farmers in small neighboring villages for generations. Within that framework, though, my father was a role model. He ventured way far away from his native village and chose a career path different from farming. He jumped into an area that no one in his family had tried. He chose to be a door-to-door salesman of tea and coffee, which, in a hot and dusty country, wouldn't seem to be a very good choice, but thankfully, Coca-Cola and cold-water freezers had not yet arrived.

My father's family counseled him against this path. "It's a bit risky," they said. "You'll be responsible for cash." Everything was paid in cash then. "You lose it or it's stolen, you're responsible." But he ignored their advice and took the job, and that propelled his life forward. Much to my parents' consternation, their son has also gone on to take risks, ignoring most of their advice. At various points in my career they've said, "What you're doing is too risky. Don't do it." I've listened and then ignored their advice and done it anyway. "There's no point talking to him," they say now, having seen that I've always somehow landed on my feet. "He's knows what he's doing. He's managed his life okay." It's funny, because by going against what was expected of him, and by sticking to what he believed was right, my father acted as a role model for me to do the same.

What else allowed me to leave home and take risks in the first place? What allowed me to do things that no man in my family had ever done? First, as I was growing up, my home life was reasonably comfortable. My family ties are strong. We're very close. This bond gave me a sense of psychological safety, which is an important concept at Google and in business. Psychological safety is an environment where you're okay as you are. You'll be given freedom and some sort of support, and you'll be loved no matter what. What fascinates me is how people who undergo trauma find this sense of safety within themselves, and I've interviewed several for this book. Some find it through nature, yoga, or meditation, all of which sustain me and have proved so effective for so many for thousands of years of recorded history.

After my initial risk of striking out on my own, I found that the more chances I took, the more confidence

I gained. This doesn't mean I didn't agonize—I didn't mortify myself. I had no idea what I was doing at first. I was fueled by going for what felt meaningful to me. What brought me joy. My risk-taking was totally experiential—trial and error. If I fell on my face, that was fine. But I learned that when you put yourself out there, when you venture out and expand your horizons, you can't fail. Because no matter what, you'll learn something.

I often talk about the risks surfers take. Most of us don't race to dive into the ocean when there's a storm at sea. But surfers do. They go toward the storm, the monster waves. They grab their boards, jump into their cars / book flights / hop on their bikes, and follow the biggest waves. It may seem crazy to nonsurfers, but it's not so crazy—this is their thrill, the challenge of leaning into the storm. It's the same with those who do free climbing. I heard rock climber Tommy Caldwell speaking on NPR the other day. Along with his climbing partner, Kevin Jorgeson, he completed the first-ever free climb of the Dawn Wall of El Capitan in Yosemite National Park. He goes all out, leans into the mountain. Nothing gets in his way. In 2001, Caldwell accidentally sawed off his left index finger just above the middle knuckle. Doctors were able to reattach it but told him he'd never be able to use that finger when climbing. So the following week, he had it removed so it wouldn't interfere with his climbing career.

MAKE A DENT IN THE UNIVERSE

Finally, it was access to information that helped me see what was possible. As I peered into the world from my parents' house, scrambling about as I tried to decide what to do with my life, I heard stories and read books and magazines about all these people around the world—historical figures or contemporary ones—who had done or were doing incredible, inspiring things. One of the earliest stories I read was about this guy named Steve Jobs and Apple computers. The article, "High Tech, High Risk, and High Life in Silicon Valley," appeared in the October 1982 issue of *National Geographic*. It featured Jobs, this young American, and other Silicon Valley pioneers.

A picture accompanying the article, which appeared in the National Portrait Gallery's "American Cool" exhibition, showed Jobs on his way to work, riding his 1966 BMW R60/2 motorcycle along a street in Cupertino, California. He wore blue jeans, a casual shirt, and no helmet. There I was, growing up in India where two-wheelers were the primary source of transportation for families, and I thought, "What's the big deal?" But the reason the article mentioned that he rode his motorcycle rather than his Mercedes was that people, at least CEOs of companies, didn't drive to work on motorcycles, and he was doing it.

But what also registered was this notion of a different kind of computer that was easy to use and had a graphical user interface, built for ordinary human beings to use primarily in their homes as opposed to engineers, scientists, and technologists in labs. This is the type of story that caught me—that helped me determine my own meaning and purpose and inspired me to take risks, push the boundaries, move forward.

So how did I go from being somewhat unhappy as a teen to being in this often blissful state I'm in now? What led to that shift? Following my inner voice, taking risks, failing miserably, meditating and practicing yoga, taking chances and falling on my face, getting up again, being curious, exploring, getting lost, finding my way, connecting with others—all have given me some level of credibility to even just talk about happiness, which I'll discuss in this book. Throughout, I'll explore paths to happiness that I've had access to in my career and life—the more data-driven approach popular with engineers and the corporate world, and the spiritual/philosopher's perspective of people such as Matthieu Ricard, the Buddhist monk who wrote *Happiness: A Guide to Developing Life's Most Important Skill*, and my good friend and fellow Googler Chade-Meng Tan, whose latest book is *Joy on Demand: The Art of Discovering the Happiness Within*. Wow. Meng, Mo, and me. That's three books on happiness coming out of Googlers. Just to add a bit more pressure on myself.

So why are multiple books about happiness coming out of Googlers? The tech industry is going through a bit of a crisis of conscience. Many have done extremely well, been a part of major transformation, and are now questioning the value and cost of what they've done. They're searching for greater meaning. I know, because I teach many of them in my class on the Internet to the Inner-net at the Esalen Institute in Big Sur, about two and a half hours south of where I live. Those familiar with Esalen probably think of such innovative radicals as Aldous Huxley, Alan Watts, Abraham Maslow, Carlos Castaneda, Ken Kesey, Hunter S. Thompson, Timothy Leary. Not techies. But in 2017, the human potential, mind-blowing, consciousness-expanding mecca of the '60s and '70s pivoted toward the corporate, recruited a new director (Ben Tauber, a former Googler), and declared a new mission—to help Silicon Valley find its soul.

"There's a dawning consciousness emerging in Silicon Valley as people recognize that their conventional success isn't necessarily making the world a better place," Tauber told *The New York Times*. "They wonder if they're doing the right thing for humanity. These are questions we can only answer behind closed doors." In the *Quartz* article, "Human Potential: The philosophy that could have stopped Silicon Valley's crisis of conscience before it started," Ephran Livini writes, "[Esalen's] new leadership is inviting ethicists and futurists to discuss the unique quandaries faced by those making tomorrow's tools." They're teaching compassion and connection, what it means to be human. To be happy.

It's the natural quest of all human beings to constantly search for higher and higher levels of meaning in life. Think Maslow's Hierarchy of Needs (which he brought to light at Esalen), where once your needs are met on one level, you can focus on the next, moving from the basic physical needs for survival to self-transcendence. If you have a successful career in tech and work in a place like Google—the freewheeling, free-thinking culture that Google creates—many of your basic needs are clearly met and you're able to let your mind go off into other higher realms. And since the general operating model of the company is to solve big problems in life to meet the needs of hundreds of millions of people, solving the happiness puzzle makes sense as it's one of the most fundamental needs of our lives. So in that spirit, perhaps those of us who've written books on happiness are also trying to tackle this problem or address our own individual take on it.

So I'm following in the wake of two hugely brilliant engineers. I'm not one of the giant brains at Google. I'm not a monk. But I can offer my own approach, which is to take from each column, toss in a bit of my own dig-deep-throw-caution-to-the-wind-this-is-who-I-am approach, then experiment and determine what works for me. I urge you to do the same.

THIS TINY LITTLE SLICE ☺F LIFE CALLED NOW

Nothing has happened in the past; it happened in the Now. Nothing will ever happen in the future; it will happen in the Now.

— ECKHART TOLLE, THE POWER OF NOW:
A GUIDE TO SPIRITUAL ENLIGHTENMENT

A few years ago, my brother told me about a vipassana meditation retreat he'd just returned from in Igatpuri, in India. He urged me to go on a retreat myself. Eager for quiet and reflection, I registered for the vipassana retreat in Onalaska, Washington.

You'd think that my time there would have been easygoing, stress-free, maybe even happy. After all, I had no meetings, no deliverables, no e-mails to respond to. Just ten 14-hour days of silent meditation. No speaking, no listening to music, no reading, no making eye contact with another human being. Just me, my body, my breath, my brain, and my mind, which then implicitly assumes my neurosis.

This was not my first retreat. I'd spent hours, days, weeks in ashrams doing yoga and meditating. I relished my times in those retreats. But this retreat was definitely the most intense. Hour after hour, day after day, immersed in the constant mental chatter that we live with—that we rarely realize is so loud. That chatter is tough to control. At least it was for me. I couldn't turn it off. I couldn't direct my thoughts in one direction or another. And when I did, after the briefest of minutes, my mind would veer left, off on a romp in a new direction, thinking about whatever it wanted to.

BECOMING FULLY ENLIGHTENED OR GOING STARK RAVING MAD

At first it was fascinating, but then I felt embarrassed, worried, and finally hopeless—I had so little control over this little chatterbox inside my head. My monkey brain at work. Hour after hour, ruminating about a friend who had not returned multiple calls, leaving me feeling ignored and slighted. Circling around to a bad quarterly review that was no longer relevant in my life. It wasn't even recent. I'd moved on. It was inconsequential, but I couldn't stop the loop. I'd focus in, manufacture nonexistent stories, conversations, scenarios in which I would lose my job, my career would become tainted—all these thoughts creating anxiety, fear, sometimes anger, and frustration.

That's how the mind works. It rarely brings up a topic that's good and celebratory to dwell on. Even if it does, it will immediately dismiss the incident as a fluke: "I just got lucky; now let's get back to the bad one." On and on and on.

Those tortured days gave me my first glimpse of the concept that you can find your happiness only in this tiny sliver, this tiny slice of life called now. Because I couldn't, or could only for a few seconds, I was clearly miserable.

My brother had told me that after about six, seven, eight days of these intense demands of watching your thoughts 14 hours a day, noticing the source of your neurosis, slowly cutting away all the excess chatter, the mind actually stills. I waited for that coveted day when my mind would still. On the sixth? No stillness. On the seventh? Nothing. On the eighth day, during my short break between the 4 A.M. and 6 A.M. meditations, I went to stretch my legs in the garden. It was a cold, damp, wintry Washington morning. Usually these mornings weren't the most pleasant, but that day, the rain, which had been constant, had stopped. The sun was coming up, peeking through the clouds.

As I walked through the garden, my mind quieted. Time stopped, yet the moment expanded, the world grew sharper.

The Pacific Northwest is a deep, vibrant green—shades from sage to emerald to lime. The land is constantly blooming, vegetation sprouting everywhere. In many ways, it reminds me of Kerala, with all the moisture. That morning, everywhere I looked, I found a new depth of color and intensity of light. The leaves on the rhododendron bushes and the holly boxwoods looked greener, more vibrant than any leaves I'd ever seen. The dewdrops on the blades of grass threw off prisms of light. I saw and heard every little detail of everything around me in a way I'd never experienced in my life. I watched the birds—a blue jay, head up, alert; a pileated woodpecker jackhammering on the bark of a Douglas fir tree; a hummingbird hovering above the branch of a Japanese maple. I'm sure I heard its wings vibrating.

I was present to all that, in that state of being fully alive, fully turned on, a state of stillness with my mind not churning. It was a state of happiness I'd never before experienced and can't fully capture in words. I started to get the wisdom of what is meant by "living in the moment." The place where you taste the richness of life, when you feel a true lasting joy, a fullness. The suchness of life. And for one brief moment, I understood. A very short window, and then it was gone. But I've never forgotten. I've always been hesitant to talk about it, because the minute I do, I'm afraid I'll start sounding like all of these mystics—Henry David Thoreau, Thomas Merton, Matthieu Ricard—who, when they speak of this type of moment, you think, *What in the hell are they talking about?*

THE POWER OF NOW

Being in the now. That moment when we leave our analytical mind behind, our ego and all its chatter, and connect with who we are, our core, our being. It's the moment in time and space where everything fades away, time stops, and nothing else matters but that moment, which is why all the great philosophical traditions focus so much attention on being present and mindful. For me, my walk through the retreat garden was my first experience with truly being in the now, a seminal turning point to finding a higher level of happiness.

While I can state the importance of being in the now with confidence, and I'm articulate about it, I have to confess that even after that amazing moment at the retreat, I still don't fully understand exactly what it means. I've always known about living in the moment—growing up in a culture immersed in yoga and meditation, how could I not? But in 1999, when Eckhart Tolle's book *The Power of Now* became a sensation, I realized how little I knew.

The first time I read the book, I only understood parts of it. I couldn't grasp what he meant by "the power of now" and, more important, why his book had become such a runaway bestseller. *What was he talking about? Doesn't the past inform the present? The present, the future?* Still, I felt obligated to plow through the book, though I struggled to get to the end. My mind swirled with elusive concepts I tried to grasp. I read it again. I still wasn't clear. I read it a third time and felt I could wrap my mind around some of the concepts. A little.

It wasn't until I started listening to some of Tolle's talks a few years ago that I started to really grasp the concept that our entire life experience only happens in this tiniest sliver of life called now. I understood that when we're in the moment—when we immerse ourselves in a piece of music, savor the taste and texture of our food, hug someone, or burst out laughing at a joke, lost in that moment of joy—all of it's happening in that one moment, now. On the other hand, if we're feeling anxious about something that happened 20 days ago, well, it happened 20 days ago. It's not now. If we're worried about what will happen tomorrow when we wake up and go to work, well, that's tomorrow. We can experience it then. Our body, our brain, our breath, our mind all work best when they're fully experiential, when we can be in this moment, now.

I got that. But I still struggled with questions. *Then how do I go about planning for my life or getting organized?*

How does anyone? Fortunately, I got the opportunity to ask Tolle himself when he came to Google to speak. I hosted the event, and while I was showing him around campus before his talk, I told him about my confusion. He might have thought I was a bit dim, but I didn't care. I wanted to understand. And who better to ask?

"Eckhart," I said, "I think I understand what you mean by living in the now, but how do I learn from the past and plan for the future?"

He looked at me as if to say, *Go on.*

"For example," I said, "at work, let's say you're sitting with your team, analyzing a project from the previous month to determine what did or didn't work. The project's in the past, but there has to be a certain amount of responsibility to conduct the postmortem analysis and learn from it. Or say you're planning for the next quarter. You're thinking thirty, sixty, ninety days ahead. You can't just think about the one second that is now. You have to think about how you'll operate and execute and get things done. In your personal life, if you're going on a vacation, you need to think about where you're going to stay three days from now when you arrive and plan what activities you're going to do five days from now while you're there. So how does all that work?"

And in his very slow, almost soporific way of speaking, with the inflections and rhythm of his German accent, one of the greatest philosophers of modern times answered my question. "Well, Gopi, the difference is between psychological time and calendar time," he said. "Calendar time is a useful construct in modern-day living. If it's January 14, it makes sense to occasionally step back from the calendar and think about what happened on January 10 to learn from our experience of that week and to plan what you'll be doing as a team during the month of March.

"But," he said, "even when you think of calendar time, reviewing the past or planning for the future, that activity takes place in the now, on January 14. We stay in the now while discussing the past or the future."

Then he spoke of psychological time, which is (and these are my words) when you project into the future or slip into the past and live in this imaginary, hellish world in your head, angry or upset about what has already happened that you can do nothing about, or about what might happen. Let's say you had a very difficult conversation. Thinking about it once, coming to some conclusions, saying, "Here's what I learned, and I'm going to move on and take this action"—that's the sensible way. Do it once, be done, then put away that whole story somewhere in the past and get it out of your mind.

But if we go back and relive that moment—and possibly also relive false moments manufactured in our head of what could have happened, what should have happened, and what could happen next—then the personal lesson is lost, and that psychological time becomes the seed of most of our anxiety, worry, and unhappiness. At that point, we have to find a way to break the cords, break the connection with that neurotic projecting into the future or obsessive ruminating about the past.

I'm now at a point where on one level I understand the detriments of immersing yourself in psychological time—worrying, say, about someone yelling at you in the past, which wasn't very pleasant, but it was three days ago, and reliving it simply causes you pain, which does you no good. That person is no longer yelling at you. That person is gone. I understand the concept.

But then, what if you're in a bad place, and daydreaming about good times helps you feel better? To help yourself get through, maybe you're reliving for the sixth time the memory of an amazing vacation you had in Tahiti or a mango you savored in the park. Is that memory experienced in the present because you're calling up that memory now? Or is it simply daydreaming? Since that pleasant moment happened in the past or may happen in the future, it's not the real experience. It's fictitious. You've flitted out of the moment. You're missing out on what's unfolding in front of you right now, which is real. This brings up a question for me: What if you're being abused or you're in a violent situation? Being present in the moment while your life is being threatened is not a portal to happiness, right?

In *Man's Search for Meaning*, Viktor Frankl, who spent three years in Nazi concentration camps, speaks of being present to intolerable pain. Based on his own experiences and those of his patients, he believed that people who found a sense of meaning, even in the most horrendous circumstances, were more resilient in the face of the suffering than those who did not. While he says that memories and goals—such as reuniting with loved ones you're separated from—can give meaning to life and increase the will to live, you also need to be present to the suffering. From that suffering can come a deeper capacity for meaning and spiritual growth. Later in this book, I return to this question about being in the now in the midst of horrific or challenging circumstances and its importance to people who've not only survived such experiences but come out the other side, filled with purpose and joy.

Sometimes being in the now is a matter of life and death. A few months ago, I watched Cirque du Soleil and was struck by how completely and totally present the artists have to be. When they're on the high wire with several people jumping from one place to another, they have to trust that everyone is fully paying attention. They can't be distracted at all. There's no other choice for them. They don't have the luxury of struggling to still their wandering minds for weeks on end in a monastery to achieve brief moments of being completely present. We can learn from the discipline instilled in surgeons, professional athletes, and artists, whose work requires intense focus. For those of us in less critical circumstances, the reward is deep fulfilment, and we can discipline ourselves, bring our minds back to the moment, by being more mindful.

Sometimes being in the now is just, well, being. Eckhart Tolle often speaks of animals in connection with being in the present. Sure, they're often in the moment when their survival is at stake, but they also know how to just be. In an article in *Unity*, "The Awakening of Eckhart Tolle," he says, "I sometimes say animals are closer to God than humans. They are closer to the source. The humans are more lost in the mind forms. Being is more obscured to the human because of the overlay of ego and mental formation."

Animals in the wild don't have a problem with being in the now. For example, if they want to go for a walk, they just get up and go. Animals that stay too close to human beings do not. Dogs, for example, can get restless, pace, scratch at the door—but their life has been forced to take on the rhythm of their human beings' life.

Tolle says that, with the exception of humans, everything in nature lives in the moment. That said, I've found if you tell people that's how all of nature lives, most will say, "It's not practical to live like that." We somehow believe that our overscheduled, overworked, overstimulated life is the only way to live. We have convinced ourselves that it is the right way, and if you don't live like that, you are living suboptimally. Sometimes when you look at the rest of nature, you've got to wonder, *Are they smarter and more intelligent than we are?*

BEING NATURALLY SMART IN AN ARTIFICIALLY INTELLIGENT WORLD

Speaking of being smarter, as I was thinking about this chapter, I read an article in *The New York Times* titled "The Great A.I. Awakening," about how the Google Brain Team used artificial intelligence to transform Google Translate and how machine learning is poised to reinvent computing itself. The team uses a concept called "neural networks." What this means is that the computers actually learn by trial and error, as human beings do. Google has incorporated this concept into its products, which have changed dramatically as a result. Google Translate, for example, "suddenly and almost immeasurably improved," according to the article. The translations are far more accurate and elegant.

Unlike humans, these machines have the good fortune of not wandering away into the future and the past the way our brains and minds do, because they are fully present and work in the context of what they have to focus on in the moment. But I wondered, from an AI perspective, what it means to be in the now. How do machines deal with distractions? And is there a creative process that is built in, or is it more a mechanistic way of functioning?

I decided to write to Mike Schuster, a senior research scientist at Google and a member of the team discussed in the article. I'd spoken with Eckhart, a top modern-day philosopher. Now I wanted to talk with someone at the opposite end of the spectrum—one of the most renowned computer scientists in the world. I'd sat next to Mike once at a Google event, both of us sitting cross-legged on the floor. I'd also thanked him after he spoke at Google's weekly TGIF meeting about language translations, the specific subject of the *New York Times* article. Both times, he wore the same pants and shoes that writer Gideon Lewis-Kraus described in his article. Here's what he wrote: "Schuster is a taut, focused, ageless being with a tanned, piston-shaped head, narrow shoulders, long camo cargo shorts tied below the knee and neon-green Nike Flyknits. He looks as if he woke up in the lotus position, reached for his small, rimless, elliptical glasses, accepted calories in the form of a modest portion of preserved acorn, and completed a relaxed desert decathlon on the way to the office; in reality, he told me, it's only an 18-mile bike ride each way."

In my e-mail to Mike, I asked, "From an AI and machine learning perspective and especially neural networks, is this meaningful at all? Do machines and AI systems have any context of being in the now?"

My understanding of neural networks is sub-basic. I understand the very basic concept, that it's an architecture based on the way neurons connect in the human brain. When I've tried to dig even the barest minimum of a bit deeper, just looking it up in Wikipedia, I've been beaten back, completely, by sentences like this one: "Back propagation is where the forward simulation is used to reset weights on the 'front' neural units and this is sometimes done in combination with training where the correct result is known." And Wikipedia then helpfully in a footnote adds, "Further explanation needed."

The article goes on to say, "More modern networks are a bit more free-flowing in terms of stimulation and inhibition with connections interacting in a much more chaotic and complex fashion," and a helpful footnote again states: "Clarification needed." Even the person who wrote this entry is lost.

At Google, I'm the least smart person in the room, which is always immediately and painfully obvious to me. This isn't my imagination; it's reality. We're encouraged to hire people who are smarter than we are. I've been with the company for 11 years. During that time, smarter and smarter people have been constantly hired, and this continues to be the case. In a company where I feel insecure about being the least smart person in the room, imagine how awkward I felt writing to Mike Schuster. For someone who operates at his level of rationality, for this highly mathematical computer scientist, the subject I'd brought up would seem like complete idiocy. (I didn't even really understand what I was asking.) When I didn't hear back, my suspicions were heightened.

A few days later, I was walking on the campus and saw Mike Schuster himself coming toward me, running in the same green cargo pants and Nikes. I thought he looked in my direction, but he didn't smile. He looked right past me and just kept running. Some of these guys at Google are not necessarily the most socially extroverted. Or maybe he had absolutely no memory of our ever having met.

I felt mortified and immediately went into my story in my head: *Oh, there goes Mike Schuster, the superintelligent human being, overindexed on his IQ, running past me, a mere mortal who works on the sales side of Google, and he must be thinking, "Here comes that stupid guy who asks crazy questions about the concept of now."* I was dreading the point where we would pass and go on in opposite directions. *He doesn't care because I'm neither artificially nor naturally intelligent as far as he's concerned. I don't even register on whatever detection system his brain is based on.*

It turns out that everything was in my head. About two weeks later, he sent me a response. He even apologized for the delay. He was very gracious and human about it all—said there'd been a lot of stuff in his in-box lately—and then he answered my question.

"This is difficult!" he wrote. "I think everybody has a different opinion. For me, personally, I don't think of humans as something entirely special; the boundaries between machines and humans are floating (for me). Of course, machines are much worse in almost all things still, but in some cases, machines are better (like playing chess or Go or adding up a huge amount of numbers). So, given that, in this sense an AI agent *can* be in the now, but others may disagree. In the future, we will see more of this and everybody will just be getting used to it I think—a machine will eventually be able to see more of the 'now' just because it can sense a lot more things and can then possibly make 'better' decisions, in whatever sense."

Wow. I think what Mike was saying is that the simplicity of "now" is incredibly complex and that, in this case, humans are ahead of machines. For now. Before signing off, he wrote, "It's a difficult topic." *He* was telling *me* it's a difficult topic. Mike Schuster, who understands back propagation, thinks it's a difficult topic. I felt completely hopeless.

A couple of days after I read Mike's e-mail, I was having lunch at Charlie's, Google's main cafeteria, and I saw him sitting all by himself. My mind working fast and furious, like a drunken monkey's, I came up with two theories about why he was eating alone: *(1) Maybe he has no friends. (2) Maybe everybody else is so intimidated, just as I am, that they don't dare go up and talk to him.* If you're a senior staff research scientist at Google, already at a stratospheric level, and the project you're working on is called Google Brain, how does it make mere mortals feel around you?

My focus shifted to his ubiquitous cargo pants. Another two theories ran through my head, which I could have asked him about and clarified but didn't dare: *(1) He owns only one pair of pants. (2) As a computer scientist, he operates with very precise efficiency and owns several pairs. Buying different clothes for different days of the week and different occasions—that takes time, time wasted. Instead, he can select the style that works for him, bookmark the website, click, and wait for the mail. If he was shopping when the site was offering a 20 percent discount, he probably figured he might as well buy 30 pairs.* This was where my mind was going, where it kept going.

Maybe he assigns a serial number to each pair. Maybe when he packs for a trip, he thinks, "I'll take 6, 7, and 10, because they're the most comfortable." Maybe before he spoke at Google, he thought, "I particularly like number 4. I should wear that to speak to the big TGIF meeting." With my mind scurrying to the places it goes to, is it any wonder I struggle with neural networks and being in the moment?

GOD SPEAKS FROM A PAY PHONE

Maybe I know more than I think I do about being in the now. I'm a diehard Burning Man devotee. Burning Man is an electronics and arts festival held once a year in Black Rock City, Nevada. Eight days of radical self-expression in this intentional community where no money changes hands. In his article in *Psychology Today*, "The Art of Now: Six Steps to Living in the Moment," Jay Dixit talks about a friend who, while at the festival, came across a telephone booth just sitting all by itself in the middle of the desert, with a sign that read "Talk to God."

When God came on the line, the author's friend asked, "How can I live more in the moment?" God's answer? "Breathe." And even though the advice seemed simplistic, the friend breathed with God and began to relax. What's interesting is that the phone booth is one of my camp's art projects at Burning Man. A camp is the community in which a group of people choose to live and work during the festival. I often work nights at the booth and play God. For all I know, I might have been God that night. In fact, I think perhaps I was. I may have been the one who helped one person to relax, to be present. For just a moment.

I fully grasp the irony of my possibly offering sage advice about being present on a fake phone in the middle of the Nevada playa. But the advice, whether mine or that of someone else in my camp, was solid. After 10 days going silently mad in the Pacific Northwest (totally worth it for those brief moments of heightened awareness), grilling Eckhart Tolle, struggling with back propagation (which I grasp only on a ridiculously high level), AI's concept of time, and Mike Shuster's cargo pants, I can now reduce the entire concept to one I can easily grasp. Breathe.

I never approached Mike Shuster that day in Charlie's, but we did begin saying hi to each other in the locker room. We don't discuss cargo pants or forward simulation. Our exchanges rely on natural intelligence, basic human courtesy, and locker-room-buddy rhythms. For example, like a kind brother, he once pointed to a few places on my face where I'd missed some shaving cream (I was on my way to the showers to finish washing it off, really).

And the other day, I finished showering and realized I'd forgotten a towel. I parted the plastic shower curtain and peered out to make sure the coast was clear before I tore off on the crazy run of shame to grab a towel. When I saw Mike was out there, I called to him, and he grinned, possibly figuring my natural intelligence wasn't keen enough to register the simple fact that I needed to grab a towel before going into the shower.

I'm sure that by the end of the day he'd built something on Google Assistant (a virtual personal assistant most often downloaded to phones and other smart devices) that can accurately predict—possibly from smell—when someone is going into the shower after a workout, then set a reminder saying, "Please, take towel from rack." Maybe he's frustrated because the app occasionally goes haywire, and instead of saying "Please grab a towel," it says something random like, "Please grab a dishrag," or "Please drop clothes in laundry." It's a bug, he'll get it fixed, no doubt.

FRIEND REQUEST— FR😊M YOU TO YOU

Take time to stop.
Stop to pay attention.
Pay attention to become aware.
Become aware to understand.
Understand to choose.
Choose to become responsible.
Become responsible to forgive.
Forgive to be charitable.
Be charitable to love.
Love to be happy.
Be happy to be free.
Be free to be infinite.
Be infinite to know God.
Know God, for that is the best there is.

— KIRSTEN CLAUSEN, "ONLY ONE LIFE"

Today, everyone's talking about happiness being a choice. Blogs, magazine articles, psychological studies, college courses. It sounds cliché by now, I know, but it's not exactly a new idea. More than 1,500 years ago, in his *Nicomachean Ethics,* Aristotle wrote that "happiness depends on ourselves." And the idea is still up for discussion. Just google "Is happiness a choice." I did and got 87 million hits. So, okay, we can choose to be happy. But then what? Countries study what makes their citizens happy and how to help them achieve that state. Bhutan, United Arab Emirates, Venezuela—all three have ministers of happiness devoted to promoting joy among their citizens. Corporations are onto happiness. Coca-Cola, Google, the Mayo Clinic, and so many others are investing millions to promote that state in their employees. Why? Because happy employees tend to stick around. They feel safer and more appreciated. As a result, they're energized, productive, confident, creative. They take more risks.

Recently my friend Karen asked me when I first realized that happiness is a choice. I would have loved to say I came in with the knowledge, but I'd have been lying. Or maybe I wouldn't have been. I probably knew it when I was very young and then forgot it as I became more enmeshed in the world. I didn't consciously think about happiness being a choice—a state achieved by employing specific skills—until the past 15 years or so, and then it wasn't through my own wisdom; it was from reading books about happiness and listening to psychologists, spiritual teachers, and engineers speak about the subject.

SATCHIDANANDA

Still, I believe I started laying the groundwork to be responsible for my own happiness when I was in high school and began going deeper into the study of Indian spirituality. I started spending time in a local ashram where they encouraged prolonged periods of silence—one day, three days, even more—and fasting. They taught us that a state of bliss and joy is our true nature, and we connect with that nature by going within. That's our choice. The term spiritual teachers use to describe this state is *Satchidananda*. In Sanskrit, *sat* means "being," "wise," "that which is." *Cit* means "consciousness," "to know," "to perceive." And *ananda* means "bliss" or "pure joy," which is our intrinsic nature. That's who we are—wise beings, part of higher consciousness, and naturally filled with bliss and joy.

Kids are completely connected with that deep sense of joy. Think about when you were a kid—at age three, four, five—or think about your own kids or kids in your life. Kids can play by themselves for hours, lost in a world others cannot see, plugged into the cosmos.

Growing up, I was given an ideal opportunity to learn to spend time with myself. Every summer, my parents shipped me off to my grandparents in their small village of Chittilamchery, where I lived with them in their big farmhouse for two or three months.

I was the only grandchild who stayed with them during those summers. For the most part, there were no other kids around. I saw only my grandparents, a few other relatives, and the people who came and worked on the farm. Things were quiet, and I spent hours by myself—watching the workers in my grandparents' rice paddies, sitting and gazing at the trees, playing, slowing to the rhythm of small village life. I was comfortable being on my own and amusing myself. Being still. Feeling joy in the stillness.

We forget that by nature we're joyful beings. By virtue of living on this planet, our intrinsic nature is coated with all sorts of impurities, layers of stories, and tangled thought processes. We can lose sight of our true nature, doubt its existence. It's like clouds masking the sun or the moon. We can't see either one. Yet if we were to part the clouds, we'd see the sun shining in a bright blue sky, the moon glowing in a field of stars. In this same way, we must clear the impurities that block our own joy and bliss, our true selves.

Going from an intellectual understanding to an experiential understanding is a long and arduous journey. Every day, we must strengthen our faith in *Satchidananda* by such activities as meditation, contemplation, compassion. Pausing to just be with ourselves. It takes a lot of trial and error and conscious experimenting. It took me a lot of both until I realized that just the experience of living our lives is a path to lead us there, to our intrinsic nature. We live our lives to find that place within, to remember and connect with who we truly are.

If we spend a big chunk of our lives looking for happiness everywhere but inside ourselves—or worse, expecting other people to create our happiness—we'll be unhappy. Since only we can make ourselves happy, those we're holding responsible for our joy are going to fall short, especially in romantic relationships, where our expectations can be so high. When they don't live up to what we expect, we can become extremely unhappy and try to change them or talk them into doing things we think will make us happy. Usually we're not going to be very successful, which makes us even more unhappy . . .

THE ELUSIVE MUSK DEER

There's an analogy in Sanskrit poetry and philosophy that beautifully captures the human condition. The analogy focuses on the musk deer, one of the rarest and most endangered species on the planet. The deer, found in Asia, notably the Himalayas, has hind legs longer than its forelegs, small tusks, and musk glands in a hairy pouch about the size of a golf ball between its navel and its genitals. These glands produce the most expensive scent in the world, worth three times its weight in gold. The scent is extremely alluring. When the stag catches the scent on the wind, he goes crazy for it. Blind to danger, he races through the forest, searching high and low, here and there, day and night, for the source of his desire. But he can never find the source of the seductive scent in the woods because it comes from within his own body.

In the article "Happiness Is Within—The Himalayan Musk Deer," spiritual teacher Paramahansa Yogananda writes of humans seeking happiness outside themselves, cautioning them not to be like the musk deer, which searches blindly for happiness everywhere but within "until finally they jump from the cliff of high hope onto the rocks of disillusionment when they cannot find the real happiness which lies hidden within the secret recesses of their own Souls."

Like the musk deer, we humans look for that treasure on the outside. We think if we just win the super lotto, get that promotion, find that mate, buy that new car or a bigger home—that's all going to lead to some sort of happiness. The sages of India have always said those things might give you a little bit of temporary happiness, but it's ephemeral. After a while, it's gone, and then you're back to seeking and searching and trying to understand. True happiness can only come from within, and until you understand that and come to peace with that, you're always going to be restless and unhappy.

Activist, author, and spiritual teacher Radhanath Swami writes of this seeking in his article "In Search of Lost Love—Lessons from the Musk Deer." He addresses our constant treasure hunt. "The true treasure lies within," he writes. "It is the underlying theme of the songs we sing, the shows we watch and the books we read. It is woven into the Psalms of the Bible, the ballads of the Beatles and practically every Bollywood film ever made. What is that treasure? Love. Love is the nature of the Divine. Beneath the covering of the false ego it lies hidden. The purpose of human life is to uncover that divine love. The fulfillment that we're all seeking is found in the sharing of this love."

Before you can share that treasure, you need to find it within—the joy, the bliss, the love. Happiness starts from the inside. To be happy, you first have to be happy with yourself, with being by yourself with no one else around, nothing to entertain you. It's a deep internal state. Until you find that place, you can't be happy with the external world. And to find that place, you first need to be present, to take time each day to connect with yourself—through meditation, a walk in nature, running, yoga—whatever works for you, however you do it.

DISCONNECT TO RECONNECT

To maintain my own sense of happiness I must do two things: First, periodically, I need to disconnect from people and external stimuli and reconnect with myself as a person. I'm unplugging to recharge, which sounds counterintuitive, but it's not. It just means tapping into a different power source. Second, I need to be comfortable with disconnecting and being with myself. And once I have that internal foundation, I can go into the outer world, fully experience that world, meet other people, and use those interactions and experiences to further my happiness.

There's a reason why mystical traditions advocate the practice of stepping outside your normal context of living—the Australian aboriginal practice of walkabout; the Buddhist traditions of leaving everything behind in pursuit of the truth, going into a retreat, or becoming a wandering monk; the Native American vision quest. Every culture has a version.

Even pop culture. The road trip qualifies. Throwing a few essentials into the trunk of your trusty car, busting out of the city limits, barreling down Route 1 from upstate New York to the Florida Keys, whizzing through the flyover states on I-80, speeding north on I-5 from Tijuana to San Francisco. Road food. Turning in to truck stops, diners, drive-ins to refuel. Day hikes. The cheap buzz of lowbrow attractions—Carhenge, The Thing, the gravity-twisted Mystery Spot, the five-story Jolly Green Giant radiating vegetable-fueled health off I-90—bizarro shrines to the absurd that absolutely take you out of the normal context of your life, and then toss you somewhere else. When you're on the road, you're in a constant state of change. Shifting scenery at every mile, a new motel or campsite every night, license plates swapping colors at every border. You meet people, have a conversation, leave them behind. Meet new people. The only thing that's permanent is you—your body, your thoughts, your breath.

You don't have to always shake up your life. You can find moments of peace and stillness even if there are people around. At Google, in the hyper-speed zip-zip-zip of it all, I find ways to hold space for myself. The other day, I had an all-day meeting with one of our biggest clients and customers, Expedia. I was moderating, so I had to be at work by 8 A.M., which meant I had to set out from home around 6:30 to get to work and prepare. From 8 A.M. to 5 P.M., I had to be completely on. I was running the whole session with 30 people in the room, including the CEO of Expedia and some of the leaders at Google. So, no pause, barely a break. Just go, go, go. Always on, jumping, facilitating, moderating, summarizing, synthesizing. It took a lot out of me mentally. I was exhausted at the end of the day, so I gave myself some space—a mini-retreat right at work.

At 6 P.M. I went to yoga class. I was surrounded by co-workers, but my eyes were closed; auditory signals from the instructor guided me through the flow, the motion, the breath. By myself. After class, I stayed in the yoga room to work on my own. I was on the floor, doing my knee-strengthening exercises for a partial tear to my ACL (anterior cruciate ligament, the key ligament for stabilizing the knee), and out of the corner of my eye I noticed another Googler, maybe in his 20s, earbuds in his ears, deep in concentration, break dancing. I didn't say "Hi." Didn't nod. Didn't acknowledge him at all. I wasn't being rude. He was in his own world, dancing jerky movements I can't even begin to name—to a hip-hop song with pretty crazy lyrics only he could hear. Then he turned upside down and stood on his head, balancing with only one arm. Going through the paces. I watched for a few seconds, thinking, *This is interesting.* Then, *It's also downright crazy. I mean, dude, why do you even do this?* Then I shrugged. And then I went back to my exercises, lost in my own world.

The point is, there were only two of us in the room, a confined space, with closed doors. And while both of us were aware of the other person, by silent mutual consent, we left each other alone to do our own thing. And were able to find the space we needed to be with ourselves.

After that, I went to dinner by myself, a ritual I often practice at Google. I go to the cafeteria and load my tray with spicy harissa-roasted tofu, zucchini with chimichurri sauce, or sesame-coconut Andhra or green bean koora; grab a physical copy of *The Wall Street Journal*; and find a quiet, solitary table in the midst of the groups of people sitting and chatting. The paper might seem like an odd choice when I could just read it on any electronic device, but it's my attempt to get away from a blue screen. I find holding a physical paper very comforting. (It probably goes back to my childhood, reading newspapers when I was growing up in India. I've always found it soothing to flick my wrist and flip the page.) I sit quietly, eat, and focus on my paper. I spend about 45 minutes. It's a way of winding down for the day.

After that day of being on nonstop, I created three, four hours of sacred space, without leaving the Googleplex. Just enjoying that time with myself. Of course, I don't always have four hours, but I still take breaks, just shorter ones. I might sneak into a conference room for 15 minutes of meditation, book a nap pod for 20 minutes, or just take a walk around campus.

At home, I do some yoga and meditate every day. Even if it's just for a few short minutes, I keep that commitment to myself. Sometimes I come home after work and just unplug. I'm lucky to be living somewhere with close access to a body of water. I often visit. I enjoy the cool breeze off the water, the lap of the small waves against the shore, the golden foothills in the background. It's amazingly peaceful and restorative. It's my Walden Pond.

Occasionally, when I feel the need to recharge, I might spend the entire weekend without seeing a single human being. I don't go anywhere. I'll go on a personal retreat in my own home, my haven, Friday night, Saturday, and Sunday alone. Maybe I'll go for a bike ride. But I don't do anything social. I live alone, so I also have the luxury of those hours of quiet with no family obligations.

Throughout the year, maybe every two months, I do all kinds of retreats to create spaciousness within. I might go on a weekend meditation retreat at the Sivananda Ashram in Grass Valley or Esalen on the Big Sur coast in California. Or I might spend a few days at a spa. Last year I visited an Ayurveda retreat in my home state of Kerala, which helped me recharge after an exhausting month of business travel.

Sometimes I take these breaks in more formal, structured retreats, like the vipassana meditation in Oregon that I wrote about earlier (as I said, this path can be tough going). Or an Outward Bound course, where I spend a week with a small group of people in the wilderness, walking, hiking, rafting down rivers, and at some point breaking off for solo trips into the wilderness.

I'm not espousing this lifestyle for everyone. It's my way. Everyone has their own way. Find the one that works for you, something that lights you up, pulls you inside, grounds you. Even if it's sitting on top of the dryer with a blanket over your head. You don't have to spend a dime.

You can get creative. Carve out time anywhere. Ten to fifteen days a month, I travel for work to New York, São Paulo, Tokyo, Dublin, Paris . . . Checking into Hotel A, getting up the next morning to present a talk on brand marketing in the digital age to one of the close to a thousand companies I do business with at Google. Then dashing to the airport, flying to City B, checking into Hotel C. Outside of work, I travel around the globe to speak about *The Internet to the Inner-Net* or the role of yoga and meditation in a world fueled with technology, or even to lead a yoga and meditation workshop.

Last November, I was in Tokyo on business. It was an intense few days of multiple meetings, back-to-back presentations, and nonstop conversation. By Friday night, I was exhausted. I had to stay the weekend because the following Monday I had another client meeting. Rather than go sightseeing around Tokyo, I chose to enter a quasi-monastic state and create a personal retreat in my hotel in the midst of the throbbing city.

That Friday night, Saturday, and Sunday, I stayed ensconced in the comfort and luxury of the Conrad Tokyo, 35 floors up, overlooking the spectacular Tokyo Bay and Hamarikyu Gardens. I meditated and read in my room; swam in the 29th-floor hotel pool surrounded by glass, looking out over the city; and went to classes in the yoga studio, where three staff members attended to me in hushed silence and extreme graciousness from the moment I arrived. I felt like an emperor every single time I went.

So in one of the largest, densest metropolises in the world, in my hotel just minutes from the fashionable Ginza district, 35 floors above the teeming crowds, I found a way to create a sacred, quiet space to be my own best friend. You certainly don't have to go to Tokyo to spend a few hours with yourself. And although it was great, it's not my usual plan. The point is to get creative and do what works for you to deepen ties with your best friend. You.

45

DON'T RULE OUT PLUGGING IN

Plugging in can also help you on your path to connecting with your natural state of bliss and joy. Sure, plugging in to the noise out there can be incredibly distracting—dozens/hundreds/thousands of your closest friends, followers, connections, all tweeting, posting, updating. You can get lost for hours chasing one link and then another to the depths of the rabbit hole, digging out only to answer the beep, ping, buzz—whatever sound you've programmed—of an e-mail, text message, request to connect, follow, friend. Until, lost in the persona you've created, driven to the edge of lunacy by the constant chatter and chasing of bright, shiny objects, you scurry under your desk, where you camp for hours, eyes shut, gnawing on your hair. So I've heard.

But we can also use the Internet and social media to go deeper into ourselves. First and foremost, that connection gives us an enormous amount of resources to study and learn from. We can find thousands of articles on meditation, stillness, yoga, grounding; links to and reviews of any book that's ever been written on any subject imaginable; mega-dozens of apps to help us instantly locate any resources we need—retreats, classes in our area, starting times, directions, where to eat after.

In going deeper, in any area you immerse yourself in, know that whatever feeling you have in the pursuit of your path—joy, sorrow, frustration, confusion, anything—you're likely not the only one to have had it. Other people have felt it, thought about it, written about it, analyzed it. They've left footprints for you. Before the Internet, social media, and phone apps, it wasn't nearly as easy to access that kind of wisdom. To learn from others, you had to travel to a conference or find a teacher, usually tucked away in some remote region.

Second, the Internet can put us in touch with a community of people who are on the same path. We don't need to go through this journey alone. In fact, it's far better if we do it with a group of people, communities and subcommunities that are forming, thriving, exchanging, and supporting each other. These networks are prolific.

And third, the Internet provides fast, instant access to whatever information you need when you need it. As I was writing the beginning of this chapter, the analogy of the musk deer popped into my head, so I searched the Internet, and three seconds later I landed on the two amazing articles by Radhanath Swami and Paramahansa Yogananda, who captured the story with far more eloquence than I could have. So, when you take personal responsibility, you can use these tools to your advantage and benefit from them. Explore the world, discover yourself, connect with like-minded others.

It's not a linear process. We have to dance our own inner rhythm. We go within, we reach out, we tap in again. To be clear, I'm not a hermit. I love engaging and connecting, and then, periodically, retreating into periods of solitude. As much as I love being social, I also like being by myself and not having to interact with anyone. Just renewing and restoring my energy. I find my sense of connection with the rest of the world, all the people out there, my interdependency with that, not when I'm sitting in a bustling coffee shop in the midst of Khao San Road in Bangkok or on Union Square in San Francisco, or when sitting in Levi's Stadium watching a 49ers game. I seem to find it best when I'm all by myself, meditating, reflecting, contemplating my own place in the universe in the context of everybody. It's a little paradoxical, I know, but there's such prismatic expansion in paradox. That seeming contradiction between point A and point B opens spaces, shifts perception, sparks knowing—*Satchidananda*. Go there. Stay awhile. And please, visit often.

TAKE Y😊UR
MEDS

*If you establish serenity and happiness
inside yourself, you provide the world with a
solid base of peace. If you do not give yourself
peace, how can you share it with others? If
you do not begin your peace work with
yourself, where will you go to begin it?*

— THICH NHAT HANH

A few months ago, I was sitting in my doctor's office for my annual physical. "Gopi," he said, "I want you to make an appointment at the South Asian Heart Center for some blood work." My brow broke out in a sweat. My heart slammed against my ribs. The doctor took one look at me and quickly said, "Don't panic. It's just blood work. Only a precaution."

Couldn't he have led with that?

Then he told me a bit about the center. It's a nonprofit, predominantly volunteer-run program in Silicon Valley whose focus is on reversing the epidemic among South Asians of insulin resistance (which increases the risk of prediabetes and type 2 diabetes), diabetes, and heart conditions. I agreed it would be a good idea to go. When I reported to the center, a kind volunteer nurse escorted me to the lab room, nodded to a chair, tied my arm, found a vein, speared it with a needle, and started drawing what felt like vats of blood, while I gazed at the bottle of anti-bacterial hand soap on the sink.

One week later—seven long days of my brain working overtime, producing endless tragic scenarios—they called. Turns out I was insulin resistant. They assured me that they had a very high success rate in turning the condition around, so I immediately signed up for their program. For less than $100 out of pocket, I received a remarkable amount of help and support—workshops, seminars, literature, ongoing sessions with Nandita, my wellness counselor, and additional consultations with nutritionists and exercise psychologists. These people were generously giving their time for a cause they believed in. They seemed happy, energized, engaged. They had definitely found their purpose.

NOT TAKING MY MEDS

At the center, they advocate the MEDS lifestyle. Not meds as in the Western medicine system, but MEDS— meditation, exercise, diet, and sleep. Take more MEDS. Right off the bat, Nandita had me alter my diet. The South Asian Heart Center encourages high-fiber plant-based foods; limited refined carbohydrates, animal fats, and processed foods; and no sugar or fried snacks. Nandita and other counselors told me that to function at a peak level, for my heart and general health to be in a terrific state, I needed to sleep seven to eight hours per night, meditate 20 minutes twice a day, and do aerobic exercise with weights for an hour at least three times a week.

I was partway there. I had a meditation and yoga practice. I did my high-intensity interval training, and of course I slept. But I wasn't hitting the numbers Nandita wanted for time spent in meditation, and my sleep fell glaringly short of the mark.

"Oh, my god," my friend Manoj said. He was in the program with me and had just received the same MEDS advice. "How can anyone fit all that in? Where's the time?"

I shrugged, then thought a minute. What they were asking seemed simple enough. Their medical research showed this is how the human body's wired. And if you think about it, nature has constructed the 24-hour day to give us the 10 hours we need to complete all these requirements. "You know," I said, "it's pretty straightforward. Invest the time, you'll function well. Don't invest the time, you won't. It's not the system's fault, nature's fault, or the medical professionals' fault that we've overloaded our lives to the point we can barely squeeze in self-care."

He didn't look at all convinced, but both of us were determined to give it a try.

On the drive home, I mulled over my new schedule. After dedicating approximately 10 hours to meditation, exercise, and sleep, I'd still have 14 hours to do all the other things I needed to do. If I couldn't fit everything in, I'd have to prioritize, let some things slide. It wasn't rocket science. Just a very natural law at work.

The easiest thing to change was my diet, though it took some extra work on my part, especially while I was traveling. Nandita recommended I track my food with a smartphone app, My Fitness Pal. I love it. I just enter what I eat and it tracks calories, sodium, fat, carbohydrates, sugar, protein—everything. You can integrate it with most activity trackers to capture your food and water intake, exercise, weight, and sleep in one place. I also use it when I'm at the supermarket, I can open the app, hold up my phone to the barcode, and immediately get a display of nutritional information that's more thorough and easier to read than the package. If I'm eating out, at least in major restaurants, I can select the restaurant, enter an item, and check out the nutrition. Then, if I want to order that item, I just click to add it to my food log.

Three months later, I sat in an exam room with Nandita, waiting to hear the results of my recent labs. "Excellent news," she said. "You're no longer insulin resistant."

I hadn't realized how nervous I was until I felt myself sag with relief. But I was going for a complete lifestyle change to minimize risk across the board. I needed to work on the other three components—consistently sufficient amounts of sleep, exercise, and meditation.

"How are you doing with your other goals?" Nandita asked. "Have you gotten in your workouts this week?"

"Oh, yes. Absolutely, pretty close. Two interval trainings and a long bike ride."

"No weights while riding, of course."

I sighed. "Correct."

"Still, not bad. Did you meditate a full 40 minutes a day and sleep seven to eight hours every night?"

I glanced at the door. "Not even once."

"Okay," she said, and we both laughed, though I wasn't all that amused. Then we started discussing why I hadn't been able to meet those goals. The main reason was that I'd been practicing my Toastmasters speeches for the upcoming international competition in Vancouver, British Columbia. Every weekday at 5:30 P.M. my coaches met me at Google. These two women spent hundreds of hours reviewing my speeches, giving me feedback, and helping me improve my performance. They showed incredible dedication to Toastmasters, and the time they devoted was just out of the kindness of their hearts.

Every weekday that I was in town, we practiced for three hours. On weekends, we practiced for at least five. Then I'd answer e-mails until past midnight. I wasn't going to cut back on my practice in order to meet my MEDS goals. The competition meant too much to me. I might not win, but I was going to give it all I had. Winning was a big dream of mine. I'd been competing in the event for 17 years. For years I'd made it to the quarterfinals, a group whittled down from an initial 30,000 entrants. I'd won the quarterfinals a few months earlier, but I still had the semifinals and finals in three months. Something had to give. Up to that point it had been the full 40 minutes of meditation, and sleep. Sleep had really suffered.

"I know the benefits of sleep, exercise, and meditation," I said. "I don't need persuading. The tasks aren't impossible, unpleasant, or difficult. You're not even asking me to swallow a foul-tasting medicine."

She smiled. I'm sure she'd heard it all.

"I should be able to do this," I said. "I know sleeping for seven to eight hours a night would do me good. And I love to sleep." So why was I resisting? This was for me, not her. This wasn't "Give me your vote" or "Give me your money." This was "I want you to sleep a little longer." And I couldn't do it. It was absurd. I knew if I slept I'd feel wonderful. I'd feel happier.

I once heard the spiritual leader Sri Sri Ravi Shankar make a brilliantly simple comment about happiness. He was giving a talk when someone in the audience asked, "Guruji, what is the way to find more happiness and peace of mind?"

"Get a good night's sleep," he said.

I looked hard at him. *That's it? If this is your most profound answer,* I thought, *why are you a great guru?* But when

I thought about it more, I realized he didn't need to go deeper because the concept is universally understood. And anyone can sleep. You don't need special skills. You just need to carve out the time. But that wasn't exactly true. Many people have difficulty sleeping. They carve out the time, lie down, and boom. They're wide awake. So I'm very lucky. I lie down, and I'm out like a light. I don't toss and turn or stay awake for hours, increasingly anxious about getting to sleep. I don't know if it's a sign of good health or if I'm so sleep deprived that any chance my body gets, it heads for oblivion.

"Gopi." Nandita touched my hand, bringing my wandering mind back. I met her gaze. "If the 40 minutes and seven to eight hours seems too much, should we set smaller increments?"

I shook my head. I didn't want to do that. The goals weren't too ambitious. I needed to come up with a different strategy. "Okay," I said, "let me commit to getting in the correct amount of meditation, aerobic/weight exercise, and sleep just once, to prove to myself that I'm capable of doing it. I can't entertain thoughts that finding the time is impossible when I've just proved to myself that it's not."

She agreed, and the very next day, I did it. I slept seven hours, did interval training for one hour, meditated for 20 minutes in the morning and 20 minutes during a break from speech practice. And that gave me the confidence that I could continue, because I'd done it once. It's similar to the first time you ride a bicycle. It proves you can do it with your own balance, which gives you the confidence to do it a second time, and a third. Then it becomes a habit, and after a while you don't even think about it. You get on a bike and go. You're completely confident riding in all sorts of conditions—uphill, downhill, surrounded by traffic. On the Google campus, I ride to meetings—one hand on the handlebar, the other holding my laptop—as I weave through Googlers on foot, skateboards, and bikes. I don't even think about the mechanics of riding. It's second nature.

So now I had the confidence to tackle my MEDS. I knew I could do it again. And I have. Not every day, but I'm definitely doing better than I was. But it was tough, especially when I was practicing for my Toastmasters competition.

MAKING PEACE WITH SAYING NO

I'd been driving myself pretty hard. Between traveling for work, speaking, attending speech practice, trying to get in my MEDS, finishing this book by the deadline so my agent and publishers didn't scream at me—which they never have, but I'm neurotic enough to believe it's coming any day now—I was a bit overwhelmed. In a good way. I loved traveling, speaking, writing, but a lot was going on, and I had to prioritize, let some things go.

I'm in the public eye, both personally and professionally. I receive requests to speak, attend functions, give a bit of my time to help with projects, and mail from people who want to connect.

I feel honored. I want to accept these invitations, reach out to those who want to connect. But I can't. So I began prioritizing the invitations I accepted, turning down engagements that weren't mandatory—parties, networking events. These are the types of things I'm going to continue to say no to, and I'm okay with that. What's harder for me is when I speak at an event, get to know the people involved, and they reach out later with a request. I can't fulfill each one, and that makes me feel awful. We all know that feeling of not having time or being too exhausted at the end of the day to return all phone calls, answer all e-mails. I love to help people wherever and however I can. I want to help everyone—I can't help everyone. I need to find a way to say no to these requests, but it's a struggle for me, and it would be much better for everyone if I'd just said no to these requests.

I was the keynote speaker at the International Nut and Dried Fruit Congress in Chennai, Tamil Nadu, India. They're a great group of people. They believe, as I do, in the health benefits of nuts and dried fruits. But their marketing strategy was archaic. My speech was to show them how they could better connect with their consumers using digital tools such as social media and YouTube. This group posted videos, but they were more for internal use—videos of past congresses in Seville, San Diego, Singapore. Nothing for their customers.

Digital media has completely transformed advertising. We live in a time when organizations, corporations, and other institutions have the ability to very directly and precisely connect with their audiences or their consumers and to emotionally engage with them in the right moment when it most matters. It's much more sophisticated and effective than the early model of shouting and trying to spam everyone. Now you can have a direct connection with the people you really want to talk to in a very precise, one-to-one manner and build a deep emotional engagement. It's a much more powerful way of connecting with the consumer. Being respectful and thoughtful.

As I talked at the nut and fruit congress, I turned to my computer, opened YouTube, and typed *walnuts*. The three huge screens lining the wall behind me displayed the search results and showed my audience the subjects being addressed in videos consumers were watching—"Top 5 Benefits of Walnuts," "3 Known Side Effects of Eating Too Many Walnuts," "Almonds vs. Walnuts: Which Nut Should You Eat?" I scrolled down the page. There were videos for recipes, face masks, exercise, stamina. These videos have racked up tens of thousands of views.

"Somebody's hijacked your conversation," I said. "You're missing a huge opportunity. One billion hours of video are watched on YouTube every single day. One billion hours. Your share of that viewing—and you represent the industry—is zero, because you don't have a single piece of content here that addresses what the consumer wants. Zero. What are you guys doing?" I asked. "You're asleep at the wheel."

They were mortified. After my speech, I met with some of the council members who worked in marketing, and we laid out a plan to develop their digital marketing brand. Since then, they've created an entire channel on YouTube with videos explaining the health benefits of nuts, demonstrating how to cook delicious recipes, and showing how to make fun gifts with nuts. They've done an amazing job. Already, they've chalked up tens of thousands of views. They've also totally revamped their Facebook and Twitter strategies, and they've tied all three together. Completely customer-focused. They've clearly established themselves as experts and a critical part of the conversation around nuts. And they're just getting started.

Not long after the videos went live, one of the members of the marketing committee sent an e-mail, which I read on my flight from Tallinn, Estonia, to Zagreb, Croatia.

On behalf of the committee, she thanked me profusely. "You inspired us," she wrote. "You really changed our thinking. Now could you please take just an hour of your time to review the videos on our channel and then give us thoughtful, constructive feedback?"

I groaned. It was so kind and sweet of them. But I had 10 files open on my desktop, and I was tap-tap-tapping away on my keyboard, with hours of preparation ahead of me for the presentation I was going to give not long after the wheels touched down. I couldn't write an analysis for her then. I knew it was just an hour. But I didn't have one extra hour to spare then. And there are a lot of other people who request an hour or two all the time. And I hated to say no. *I can't say no,* I thought after reading that e-mail, *but I could say no to doing it at that moment or even within the next few days.*

I quickly shot her a note, thanking her profusely for her kind words. Then, "I'm on the plane, traveling. Let me take a quick look after I get home." Unfortunately, with my speech practice, book, MEDs, work, flying, and personal events, I never found a moment to look. It would have been so much better for everyone if I'd just explained that my schedule was too packed to meet this request, but instead, because I hated saying no and seriously wanted to help, I pushed the review off for a few days, hoping I could get to it, and then let it slide. I'm not okay with having let it slide. I still feel terrible.

WHEN JUST CONNECTING IS ENOUGH

When I speak, people seem to feel a connection with the content, which means so much to me—to get my message out there and have people connect with it. But I always feel I need to do more, reach out, connect on a deeper level, even when it could come at the expense of connecting with and taking care of myself. And when I can't, I feel guilty, which zaps all resources and does no one any good.

I recently returned from Memphis, where I spoke to 1,300 people—employees of St. Jude Children's Research Hospital and the fund-raising arm of their organization, American Lebanese Syrian Associated Charities, or ALSAC. It was a Google event, and they're clients. I'm in awe of how much they give and all they accomplish.

Their chief marketing officer had read my book, which is why she'd wanted me to speak, not about technology or digital brand building, but about *The Internet to the Inner-Net*. I couldn't believe she'd read my first book *and* had connected with it enough to want me to speak for an hour about employing practices from ancient wisdom traditions, such as meditation and yoga, to balance and deepen the exciting strides occurring in technology, rather than unplugging and shunning tech altogether. Because more change is on the way, and we need to prepare ourselves and our children for a future in which technology plays a much bigger part. We can evolve together.

My good friend Soren Gordhamer, founder of Wisdom 2.0, is dedicated to addressing "the great challenge of our age: to not only live connected to one another through technology, but to do so in ways that are beneficial to our own well-being, effective in our work, and useful to the world." Those who speak at his conferences around the globe are also part of the movement, as are the thousands and thousands of participants who attend these Wisdom 2.0 conferences, workshops, and meetups.

I was excited to share these views with St. Jude, an amazing program. This nonprofit hospital treats children with catastrophic pediatric diseases. Since they opened their doors in 1962, treatments created at St. Jude have helped push the overall childhood cancer survival rate from 20 percent to 80 percent. People from 80 countries have brought their children there. And no bill is ever sent to these families for treatment, or travel, or housing, or food. So even as the U.S. government goes through all its crazy machinations in D.C. about health care reform, Obamacare, and funding, these people are quietly doing their good work. What a humbling honor to go speak to 1,300 people who raised $1.3 billion last year to cure cancer, or to help treat cancer, for young kids and their families. What an astonishing model. Talk about creating happiness in such a meaningful way.

The hospital was founded by the comedian Danny Thomas, a Catholic from Lebanon, whose favorite saint was St. Jude. When he was just starting out in the entertainment industry, he was broke. The day before his son was born, he walked into an empty church, dropped his last $7 into the offering box, and prayed to St Jude. Thomas promised that if the saint helped protect and take care of him, he'd build a shrine to him. That same week, he landed his first big comedy gig, paying about $70, 10 times the amount he'd put in. After that, his career took off. Keeping his promise to St. Jude, and believing that "no child should die in the dawn of life," Thomas traveled around the country persuading people to help him build this hospital. He gave, and gave, and gave.

Well, as I talked, they really connected with the material and gave me three standing ovations. I couldn't believe it. These people who have changed children's lives for almost 60 years, who give so much of themselves, are so interested in the inner-net and are blending that to more responsibly work with technology, to go deeper into who they are as the world becomes increasingly automated and communities become increasingly virtual.

"Thank you," I finally said. "I'm humbled by the work you guys do. You save lives every single day, quietly, and most people don't even know you're doing it. You've defied gravity. You've found the solution to a problem the mighty U.S. government hasn't been able to solve—how to provide low-cost health care. And you've gone one better. You provide *free* health care, and if curing cancer is used as a metaphor for the impossible, you're doing it."

At the end of the conference, as I was leaving, a woman came rushing up to me and introduced herself. Her name was Roxanne. Excited by the speech, she'd just called her son and told him to read *The Internet to the Inner-Net*, to connect to his own inner-net. "We'll do it together," she'd told him.

When I returned to Silicon Valley, my in-box was full of requests to connect on LinkedIn or to friend on Facebook, all from those who'd connected with the content of my speech. I accepted them all, and that's really all that's required, but I would have liked to answer each one, acknowledging our connection and thanking them for their kind words. But I can't, so in this case, I need to make peace with yes being enough, which is always much easier when I've given the time to taking care of myself first. Then I can my struggle from a distance, with more insight and calm. So we're back to it once again—MEDS.

WHAT I CAN'T MAKE PEACE WITH . . .

I'm okay with not attending events where my presence isn't at all required, and I'm making peace with not attending those I'd love to attend but just can't. But I still can't make peace with—and I don't think I ever will—not being able to respond to all the messages that come in.

I've had to prioritize what I respond to. Sometimes that's fine. In many cases, such as with certain requests to speak, if I don't respond, the group will just move on to one of 50 other potential speakers on their list. It's not a big deal for them if I don't get back to them. But it is to me, and I'm trying to make peace with not responding to those requests.

What's harder are the requests where people are reaching out to me specifically from other countries such as India, Singapore, and Saudi Arabia. When I can't attend, which I feel bad about, I should still get back to these people, but that requires a few hours a night. I could decide to simply not attempt to respond, but that seems so rude and insulting. I could just shoot a brief form letter, "I'm sorry. I just don't have the time," but that seems as though I'm so full of myself. So I struggle with (a) turning down requests and (b) not being able to reply to each one in the eloquent, gracious manner I feel they deserve.

Then there are those individuals who reach out because they've been moved by a speech I gave, an article I wrote, or my first book. I can't make peace with not having the time to respond to each message, which I feel is only courteous. Plus, I want to express my appreciation for their messages, express my joy that they want to go deeper within.

But I just can't respond to all the input coming from all channels—e-mail, Facebook messages, text messages. My habit has always been to stay up until I've cleared them all out, often until one, two, three o'clock in the morning, fighting sleep, then going to work the next day tired. I can't do that anymore. I can't and won't sacrifice my sleep, exercise, and meditation. Sacrificing these runs completely against the very practices I advocate of self-nurturing, being your own best friend, going deeper into your true joy. Who can be open to joy when they haven't slept, eaten well, had some quiet time, moved their bodies, and focused on their breath?

We all have busy lives. We all need to take care of ourselves. Otherwise, we can't go deeper, find our true nature, our joy. And then we're no good to ourselves or others. It's a challenge, one I haven't yet figured out. But I'm working on it. I do realize now that I can't neglect my MEDS, and I encourage everyone to take theirs. If we each did this, focused on connecting with our true selves, if we all became happier as a result, even if it was just a few at a time, think of how our planet would change.

THE W☺RLD IS A VERY LARGE PLACE

Gradually, as our perspective deepens, we begin to experience our own lives in the context of a wider purpose. We begin to look at all our melodramas and our desires and our sufferings, and instead of seeing them as events happening within a lifetime bounded by birth and death, we begin experiencing them as part of a much vaster design. We begin to appreciate that there is a wider frame around our lives.

— RAM DASS

In this vast world of ours, we have so many opportunities and choices, so many roads crisscrossing, looping back, running parallel, paving so many routes to we-pray-we-know-when-we-get-there. To navigate this journey, to deepen your perspective, you have to know your true north, your life's purpose. When you do, everything else in your life aligns with it. And that alignment brings deep joy. On a very simple level, that alignment means knowing what to say yes to in your everyday decisions— knowing where you want to focus your attention, spend your time, devote your energy. It means the people you hang out with, the books you read, and the organizations you support. If you take it one level higher, it's that true north sense of purpose that allows you to get out of bed every single day and gives you the motivation to solve problems in a big way because you're fired up by it.

And in the highest, truest sense, that sense of purpose is what allowed someone like Mother Teresa to leave the comforts of her position as headmistress of the Loreto Convent School and journey into the streets of Calcutta to work with the poor. She received what she termed her "call within the call." She said it was an order. "To fail would have been to break the faith."

FIND WHAT LIGHTS YOU UP

Aristotle said, "Where the needs of the world and your talents cross, there lies your vocation." My central purpose manifests in professional self-expression, drawing on my interests and talents, my skill set, given my formal education, training, experience, interests, and passion. It falls squarely at the intersection of two areas: the world of digital technology and the world of business. The questions that drive my mission are: How can we use the power of business organization and the power of technology to change life on this planet for the better? Can harnessing this power serve to empower people? Can it change the quality of life for people? Tackling these questions is what I enjoy most about being in a place like Silicon Valley, working at a place like Google. I still can't take for granted the fact that all publicly available information, knowledge, and insights are now easily accessible to every single human being from a little device we keep in our pocket or bag. Most of this information is free. For instance, no one's charged for viewing the amazing works of art from more than 500 museums and art galleries around the world that the Google Art Institute makes available to the world to enjoy on their laptops, tablets, phones. This access has leveled the playing field on the planet. It's changed our lives.

I also get a deep sense of mission and purpose from being happy. Just being a happy human. I feel that a primary purpose in each of our lives is to find our own way to happiness, discover our own talents, and then use those talents that bring us joy as best we can. Foster them, nurture them, grow them both for the greater good and, more important, simply for the joy and delight of practicing them. I also find a deep sense of purpose from studying ancient wisdom teachings, practices such as yoga and meditation—exploring and learning from them, then sharing whatever I find useful with others.

PURSUE WHAT MATTERS TO YOU

When I started out in the business world, my sense of meaning and purpose was different from what it is now. The fulfillment I find in being a happy human, the sense of mission and purpose I get from practicing and teaching yoga and working at the intersection of technology and business for the greater good, had not emerged. I had some notion of maybe wanting to grow a business, but at that point I was still thinking of it in a very narrow, crass, material kind of way: *Wouldn't it be cool? Think about how much money I could make. There have to be lot of perks, right?*

Although I had a vague notion of what I wanted to do with my life, what I wanted to experience, I was very clear that the world was much larger than the little bubble I lived in, my little pocket environment. I knew if I could live in another country or take time off to roam the world, it would open up a lot for me. That's what lit me up. Except I had no means by which to do it. So after earning a graduate degree in business administration from the Indian Institute of Management, I started looking at jobs internationally. I was open to going just about anywhere.

As I've said, once you set the intention, doors magically open. In this case, two Hong Kong–based companies were advertising for people with technology skills from India. At that time, to learn about and access these opportunities you needed to be living in one of the big metro cities like Mumbai or New Delhi, where they advertised the interview process in the local papers. I was lucky enough to live in New Delhi, so I was able to interview there.

I was hired by Hutchison Whampoa, a huge conglomerate, as a software analyst. The specific business I worked for was A. S. Watson, a retailing giant in southern China, the equivalent of Walgreen's, Kroger, or Safeway, with stores all over Hong Kong, Singapore, Malaysia, and Taiwan. I loved that job, and even more, I loved living in Hong Kong, loved the full experience of expressing my adulthood. I had moved. I was working internationally. I was being exposed to so much that was new. I was working with people from around the world. I was making decent money. Professional and cultural experiences were opening up. All that learning and eye-opening possibility made me feel alive, excited. Traveling, exploring something new, being curious—all that still makes me feel that way.

FINDING MY WAY

True to my determination to discover the world, after three years in Hong Kong I moved once again, this time to San Francisco. After working at a couple of companies there, I enrolled in the Wharton Executive MBA program at the University of Pennsylvania. After that, I lost my way a bit. There's a lemming-like behavior in graduate programs that drives you in certain directions, and you go in one of those directions because everyone else does. In the top business schools, strategy consulting and investment banking are two big career drivers. Both are legitimate and worthy things to do. So, after Wharton, I went into consulting.

I worked at McKinsey & Company. It's an incredible firm; I had warm, funny, whip-smart colleagues; and I benefited greatly from my time there. But did I take a job there because I was really driven to do that kind of work long-term? No. In some ways, I was beginning to feel like a professional tourist, dropping into companies, giving them a little bit of advice, leaving, moving on to the next one. I was helping these companies build their business, but I felt as though a part of my soul just wasn't engaged. I wasn't feeding it. Instead, I was doing the work because of external motivators: It was prestigious and good for my career. And sure enough, because of that, I didn't last very long.

I left after a year to work at a tech start-up, yet even that decision was driven by the glamour of building a start-up company as opposed to any intrinsic love of being a builder, entrepreneur, tinkerer. There are so many professional choices I've made where I had to muddle my way through because I wasn't completely clear about why I was doing it. I worked at two start-ups, both great learning experiences. I was definitely engaged and learning— writing business plans, raising money, building the business, hiring people, training, motivating. Both were moderately successful, both were sold in modest deals. But start-ups require infinite patience and a willingness to hang in for the very long term. And looking back, that was something I wasn't fully prepared for. None of those jobs captured my spirit, but they did give me some of the business foundation I needed to do the work I do now.

CREATE A PLAN B

Few of us pop into this world knowing exactly why we're here, what we're here to do. It takes time, some trial and error. Until you find your purpose, you'll make moves in the right direction and the wrong direction. You'll need to do some exploring to figure out what fits. Keep your antenna up for what gives you that spark. You'll have to center yourself, friend yourself, and learn who you are. You'll need to take a few risks to figure it out. You'll need to take action.

I've learned that there are three important points to remember when taking action. First, you need to have a very strong reason for taking that action. In my case, when I moved to Hong Kong and San Francisco, I wanted to learn about the world. Second, you have to be able to generate some sense of excitement about that action. After a while, I knew the job at McKinsey wasn't feeding my soul. You want to pay attention to that lack of resonance. You deserve to find what you love and create a life that supports that. To be happy on the deepest level. Third, while you might be afraid to consider it, things could go wrong when you take action, so look at all possible outcomes.

Have some concept of the worst that could happen, and draft an exit plan for what to do if it does. This is your plan B. These three steps can greatly ease any fear of failure you may have.

Here's an example of a plan B. When I was in my 20s, I quit a very stable, secure, well-paying job in Hong Kong to move to the United States, where I had no job. As I've mentioned, my father grew up in an era when people stayed in one job for their entire careers. You just didn't switch. Once you got a job, you stayed there. For 35 years he worked for the same company, slowly climbing the ladder, one rung at a time. When I came home before leaving for San Francisco and told him my plan, he was completely astonished. "You quit your job?" He shook his head, clearly at a loss. "Do you have another job?"

"No." Not only did I not have another job, but I didn't have a country. I'd sold everything, packed what I needed, and was moving to a new country with $7,000 in my pocket, no authorization to work there (no work visa), and no place to live.

My dad tried his best to be supportive. He was proud of my initiative. "So, what are you going to do?"

"I'm going to try to get a job."

"What if that doesn't pan out?"

"Then I'll go to Australia," I said. "If that doesn't work out, I'll try Singapore. If that doesn't work, I'm going to Dubai. They need my kind of skills. If Dubai doesn't work, I'll come back to Mumbai and start rebuilding again. I'll figure something out."

That was my attitude. One way or another, I'd somehow find my way. Among those five options, I was sure I'd be fine. Of course, at that time I was young and didn't really know the difference between success and failure. I just felt

I could do it, and my brazenness was helpful. When you're older, you might know the difference between success and failure, but you've also had more experience with both, so you can draw on that to ensure you'll land on your feet. Just listen to yourself, search for what resonates, what makes you hum. Try plan A, prepare a plan B, and head north. Circle. Overshoot. Circle back. Home in. Home in again. You'll get there.

PART II

REWRITE
Y😊UR
STORY

We have a philosophy at Google called launch and iterate, where even before a product is perfected, it's put out there so people can work with it, try it, play around with it. Then based on their feedback, the next version of the product is launched. Then we do it again. And again. The iteration before the newest one wasn't a failure but a door to new possibilities, new problems solved. My personal mantra is that all of life is one giant experiment. And experiments yield unexpected results—some miraculous, some left of center, some seeming duds. There's something incredibly empowering about seeing each effort as an iteration, a deep self-exploration, an opportunity for growth, a chance, each time you fall, to bounce back. Think about the possibilities for incorporating this philosophy into your life.

WHEN LIFE CRUMBLES

I honor the place in you where the entire universe resides. I honor the place in you of love, of light, of truth, of peace. I honor the place within you, where, if you are in that place in you, and I am in that place in me, there is only one of us.

— ANCIENT SANSKRIT BLESSING

How do you find happiness in the middle of an extremely painful situation such as death? This was the challenge I faced when my father passed away and I found myself in a vacuum, desperately searching for something to hold on to.

On August 1, 2017, a Tuesday, my mother called from India. "Your dad has a fever," she said. "He's awake, but dazed. He's mostly silent and not responding much at all." When I called back later, she said the doctor had stopped by the house. He thought my dad might be weak because of a sodium deficiency and felt it would be better to take him to the hospital to give him drips, perform some tests, and observe him more closely.

My father had had a fall a few years earlier that left him paralyzed from the neck down until he regained partial control of his body. He went from being able to function

independently—drive a car, take a walk—to being dependent on someone to take care of him. Whenever he'd had
problems in the past and I'd asked if I should come home,
my mother always said, "You're so far away. Don't worry.
If it's very serious, we'll let you know, but we'll manage
here." But on this day, my mother said something she'd
never said before. "Come home for one day and see him,"
she said, "and then you can go back. I know you're super
busy with your upcoming international speech competition and your work, but just come home for one day, Gopi.
Just one day." This time her intuition told her I should go,
and with a feeling of sadness, dread, and purpose, I told
my colleagues I'd be leaving for India the next day.

Then I called my brother, who'd already arrived in
Trissur, in Kerala, my home state. He would have met with
the doctors, and I wanted to get his assessment of the situation. "He's in intensive care," my brother said. "They've
run some tests. Dad hasn't had a stroke or anything that
serious, but he does have pneumonia, which the doctors
feel they can beat." We were both quiet. My father was 91,
and we both knew pneumonia can be fatal for the elderly.
"You should come right away," he said.

After I hung up, I punched in my travel agent's number and asked for a flight the next day on Emirates via
Dubai, the fastest route from San Francisco to Kerala.

"I can fly you out on Thursday," she said, "or maybe
tomorrow, but on Singapore Airlines."

"No," I said. "It has to be Emirates. And tomorrow. I
need to leave tomorrow."

"The flight's full. It's summer, Gopi. You know what
that's like. Parents and kids—all going home to visit
relatives."

She sounded frustrated, exhausted by families book-
ing flights, cars, hotels, shuttles. I didn't know how far I
could kindly push her, but I was desperate. "Keep looking.
Please. I have to get home." I felt such a sense of urgency,
frustration. If she would just keep looking . . .

For the next half hour, both of us stayed on the line—
with her searching on her end, me searching on mine—
until she said, "We're in luck! I found one seat on an
Emirates flight leaving tomorrow."

"Put me on it," I said.

"Done."

I hung up the phone and sighed. I think I'd been holding my breath the entire 30 minutes. After that, I felt alter-
nately anxious and sad. I had to get to my dad. I wished I
could beam myself up and over to Trissur. Unfortunately,
I didn't have that ability (yet). So the next day, I boarded
the flight, and 24 hours later, on Thursday, August 3, I
landed at 4 A.M. local time, reached home three hours later,
and took a short rest until visiting hours started at 10 A.M.
When I got to the hospital, my family was gathered in the
waiting room outside the ICU. I was told that my dad was
conscious, very lucid, and he'd been talking. Before I went
in to visit him, a nurse brought a special pair of shoes for
me to wear into the ICU. I entered the unit, pushed aside
the curtain surrounding my dad's bed, smiled down at
him, and slipped inside.

He looked much older, frailer than he had a few
months earlier. It was shocking to see him like that. At
the same time, it cracked my heart wide open to see my
dear sweet dad, my hero, so vulnerable, so innocent. His
eyes lit up when he saw me, I bent down and hugged him
carefully, and when I finally let go, he pushed aside his
oxygen mask and immediately asked me how my practice

was coming for the upcoming speech competition, which was three weeks away. "It's going very well," I said, my voice catching. We ended up having a loving, warm, and meaningful conversation despite his nasal feeding tube and oxygen mask shoved to the side. He joked with me. We laughed. He told me that my shirt—a striped dress shirt in lavender and white—looked good on me. I'm so grateful we had that time.

When I came out of the ICU, my brother told me I had to go back in to return the special shoes. I went inside, returned the shoes, and on my way out saw that they hadn't yet closed the curtains around my father's bed. I glanced toward him. He must have felt me there because he looked up at me, smiled, and waved. I smiled and waved back, my heart lifting. I loved him. He was my hero.

By that point, despite living in six different places around the globe, the entire extended family had arrived— all the kids and their spouses, all the grandkids. One by one, our immediate family had time with my father. I don't think we realized that for each of us, this was going to be the final conversation. That evening at seven o'clock, my father passed away peacefully, with my elder sister and younger brother each holding his hand. During those final minutes they spent with him, they said he didn't appear to be conscious. He looked peaceful, sleeping, breathing normally. But sitting there, holding his hands, their eyes glued to the monitor, they saw his breathing slowing, his oxygen level decreasing, and then his heart rate leveling out until it stopped.

Studies show that although 80 percent of Americans would rather die peacefully in their homes surrounded by friends and loved ones than in a highly sanitized hospital among scrub-wearing strangers, only 20 percent do.

Although I can't find a similar study in India, I feel certain my father would have wanted to die at home, but since he couldn't, we brought home to him: our family. I'm so glad we were all able to come to see him, to spend time with him before he died, to be with him. I'm so glad he was lucid and talking with us and that his passing was comfortable and peaceful rather than traumatic. That brought us all a deep sense of peace and joy.

PAYING TRIBUTE TO MY FATHER

On Friday, after an all-night vigil at home and before his cremation that evening, we held a daylong memorial with extended family and friends. Everyone was crying. Our culture has a very public and community-supported grieving process, which is actually extremely cathartic. My father touched the personal and professional lives of hundreds of people, who came to pay their respects, each arrival leading to another massive bout of sobbing. But in the midst of it all, there was a sense of joy, happiness, peace, and deep satisfaction knowing that my father's long life had been well lived.

Here was someone who grew up in a poor Indian village, had one set of clothing to wear to his rural village school (to which he walked barefoot), where he received a modest 10 years of education. Despite those circumstances, he learned to speak seven languages, started out as a door-to-door salesman of tea and coffee and rose to become an executive of a multinational company. And along the way, he supported the education of his four kids, who collectively earned 10 degrees. Our family felt a deep sense of pride in who he'd been, a sense of celebration for all he'd done.

Before my brother and I lit our father's body, I bent down, kissed his forehead, and said, "Thank you for giving me life. I'll make you proud." I felt a deep sense of peace and purpose in life, and this continues, as a part of him. His energy and his teaching continue through us. After his cremation, we felt a sense of closure, and this—after the initial shock—is when the loss hit and the true grieving set in. Our entire family stayed together in my parents' small house for 10 more days to grieve my father's passing, celebrate his life, support one another, and perform last rites as per our cultural traditions.

Surrounding yourself with a network of positive, supportive people is important during times of great loss. And it goes both ways. In the *New York Times* article "How to Build Resilience in Midlife," Dr. Steven Southwick, a psychiatry professor at Yale Medical School and coauthor of *Resilience: The Science of Mastering Life's Greatest Challenges*, says, "Any way you can reach out and help other people is a way of moving outside of yourself, and this is an important way to enhance your own strength."

This was true for my family. Brothers, sisters, spouses, kids, and my mom, huddled together, grieving and occasionally crying, remembering him. Yet at the same time, being there for one another, supporting one another, feeling that we would hang together through it all.

THE IMPORTANCE OF SUPPORT

So many people have held out a hand to me since my father's passing, and I've reached back to everyone. Some people have offered extreme amounts of kindness, some people just the most marginal amount. But it doesn't matter. The tiniest acts of kindness, of acknowledgement, even if only a small note left on my door, I deeply appreciate. Every bit counts. When life crumbles, my advice would be this: Don't cut yourself off. Reach out to all of those who hold a hand out to you. Receive the positive, supportive energy and gratefully accept it.

Jennifer Wesley, a colleague and friend, sent a beautiful note to me. She opened the note with "I have not been through the experience of losing a parent, but having witnessed my husband's journey after losing his father, I can only imagine the pain and grief you're experiencing. I am bringing with me to Mountain View a copy of Joan Didion's *The Year of Magical Thinking*. You can read it when you're ready. It's beautifully written and raw, and skewers so much of what we are told about what grief looks like—what processing loss looks like. Joan Didion wrote this book chronicling the year following her husband of nearly 40 years, John Dunne's, passing."

Jennifer included a passage from the book:

This is my attempt to make sense of the period that followed, weeks and then months that cut loose any fixed idea I had ever had about death, about illness, about probability and luck, about good fortune and bad, about marriage and children and memory, about grief, about the ways in which people do and do not deal with the fact that life ends, about the shallowness of sanity, about life itself. I have been a writer my entire life. As a writer, even as a child, long before what I wrote began to be published, I developed a sense that meaning itself was resident in the rhythms of words and sentences and paragraphs, a technique for withholding whatever it was I thought or believed behind an increasingly impenetrable polish. The way I write is who I am, or have become, yet this is a case in which I wish I had instead of words and their rhythms a cutting room, equipped with an Avid, a digital editing system on which I could touch a key and collapse the sequence of time, show you simultaneously all the frames of memory that come to me now, let you pick the takes, the marginally different expressions, the variant readings of the same lines. This is a case in which I need more than words to find the meaning. This is a case in which I need whatever it is I think or believe to be penetrable, if only for myself.

I was so moved by her elegiac tone, the longing, the urge to collapse time—no before, no after—just a lifetime of slight variations on the same moment, extending it. During those 10 days following my dad's cremation, and after, specific moments around his passing and the ceremony that followed came to each of us and made us particularly sad. For my mom, one of these memories was created just before he was cremated. In our tradition, one by one, each person circles the body and then lies prostrate in front of it. When it was my mother's turn, my sister went with her, holding her. As they circled my father, my mother, fighting back tears, glanced back. It was her last look at her beloved husband's face, and the memory was heartbreaking and overwhelming. The memory that kept coming up for me was my father's smile and wave as I quietly left the ICU. At that moment, I thought, *Okay, he seems so much better. I'm going to see him again tomorrow.* But that turned out to be his final smile and wave, saying goodbye, forever.

My friend Sriram wrote a two-line note. His generosity and his uplifting words about happy memories helped penetrate my sorrow. "Nothing prepares you for a moment like this," he wrote. "When I lost my mother, someone told me that losing a parent is like losing an axis of your life. You never really get over it, yet memories of happier occasions do tend to surface over time. Please let me know if we can help in any way here. Later, Sriram."

MY THREEFOLD PLAN FOR HAPPINESS

As I write this, for the first time in my life, I'm going through the process of grieving for a parent. And it is a process. I've never felt this way before—everything flat, dulled, muted, the way my friends who suffer from depression have talked about feeling. But I know I'll get through it. One thing that helps is a strong sense of connection with my father. Friends of my family have written to me telling me how much I look like him. "I look at his photograph," one friend wrote, "and you've got the same cheeks, the same smile."

Hearing those words, or variations on them, brings me a sense of closeness to my father, a sense of continuity. I carry within me the seeds of my father, my grandfather, my grandmothers, and all the lineage that somehow flows through. Scientists talk about genetics—hair color, skin color, height, bone structure. But there's more than that. There's also a sense of wisdom and life skills passed on through many generations, all flowing through you. This is one of the great cosmic mysteries of life, this passing on of knowledge and inner and outer traits. We don't stop to ponder it often, if ever, but somehow in each of our bodies are the seeds of somebody who lived 400 years ago, and much further.

While I was in India and after I came back, I wanted to face and experience my grief, and I also wanted to find my way back to happiness in the midst of this loss. I'm focusing on three pieces: remembering our life together, celebrating my father's life, all the amazing things he did, and saying to myself, however often I need to, *Now it's your responsibility. The mantle has been passed on to you. He set an example for us. He came very far. He made the best of his life. What can you do to continue that tradition?*

This philosophy is working for me, and I offer it to you. Death is part of life. And though I dearly miss my father's physical presence, I feel him with me. It is sad and sweet, but I am at peace leaning into the situation with ease, grace, and power and celebrating the life of a remarkable man who gave me my own life and who was and always will be my hero. And somewhere in the process of reframing, I was able to step away from sadness into a portal of happiness.

WHEN
Y😊U FALL,
BOUNCE

Our deepest fear is not that we are inadequate. Our deepest fear is that we are powerful beyond measure. It is our light, not our darkness, that most frightens us. We ask ourselves, "Who am I to be brilliant, gorgeous, talented, fabulous?" Actually, who are you not to be?

— MARIANNE WILLIAMSON, *TALES FOR TRAINERS*

Not long before I started working at Google, my life fell apart. In one week my relationship ended, I was laid off, and my living situation was uncertain. I slouched around my just-sold house (decluttered of all traces of me) in a ratty Wharton T-shirt and sweats, holding on for dear life to my cup of masala chai. Mind-fogged, boot-in-the-gut debilitating days. After about 10 of those days, I shook myself. I had to do something to shed this temporary loser identity before I began to truly buy into it. I rose from the semi-dead, pulled on a pair of jeans and a rugby shirt, drove to an orientation event at the Silicon Valley Triathlon Club, and immediately joined. But before I could attend meetings, show up for training sessions, or

HUMAN

whiteboard future triathlon opportunities, I received an invitation from someone I barely knew to stay with him and his family in Iceland. Having never met, Pamrod and I had exchanged only a few e-mails following an introduction through a mutual acquaintance.

I've always believed that when a crisis descends, you can drown in it or you can reframe it and see opportunities. So instead of contracting into a place of why-me-life-sucks-I'm-going-to-winter-in-my-closet (which I'd soon be without), I decided to put my triathlon plans on pause and accept my friend's invitation—to be curious, reach out, expand, adopt the attitude that the universe was pushing me in a different direction and go with that.

Then there was the two-pronged synchronicity I couldn't ignore. First, if at any other time someone I'd randomly met had said, "You have to come to Iceland and stay with us," I would have said, "I don't have the time. With all that's going on in my life (and I'm sure you can relate to this), it's hard to fit it in my schedule. Also, I have to be really careful about my vacation days, so I can't come." But suddenly, I didn't have a job. I could go anywhere, and I might as well take the opportunity.

Second, seemingly by chance, I heard on the radio that Icelandair had launched new service between Reykjavik and San Francisco—a direct flight for $400 if you booked a midweek flight online, which I rarely did. For non-business travel, I usually flew out on Thursdays and returned on Sunday or Monday to preserve my vacation days. But without being employed, I didn't have to worry about vacation days. I could go anytime.

Now Iceland is cool and hip, but back then, no one was saving up to take a big vacation in Iceland. Still, I was intrigued by the improbability of it all. *Why not Iceland?* From everything I'd read it sounded intriguing, so why not?

Going with the intrigue of the improbable, taking off in a direction that's completely unexpected, asking yourself *Why not?* are huge keys to happiness. You're not planning, but it's serendipitous, the circumstances are right, so you go for it. That's what life is about, and as long as you keep your curiosity, adventure, and exploration going, you'll always find a certain amount of intrigue, interest, and joy in your life.

GO OFF THE RAILS

I had decided on Iceland, but then it came to me— why not explore further? I had the opportunity. But how would I get by? I had a six-week severance package, which wouldn't go far. I also qualified for unemployment, but I didn't want to apply. I'd been raised with the notion that going on the dole meant you'd really gone off the professional rails. Forever. You couldn't care for yourself. You were dependent on government largesse. I had a ridiculous story in my head that collecting unemployment meant my life had completely stopped functioning; I'd stopped functioning. I'd gone from engineering school to a top business school to leeching off the state. Weave into that narrative everything I'd heard or read about in public discourse and in incendiary politicians' speeches against jobless immigrants filtering through our borders, pushing up unemployment, and becoming a drain on society—no.

I didn't want to be that person. I wanted to be the hardworking person who gives back. When I shared my thoughts with a friend, she said, "No, no, Gopi, don't feel too bad. You've been working hard, paying into this

THE HAPPY

insurance plan every month. This is your money. You can collect it." So I applied for unemployment. Thanks to the Internet, I'd be able to dutifully apply for jobs every week. I was in all the databases that recruiters accessed. They could reach me anytime, anywhere. I'd check my mail religiously. If someone wanted an interview, we could video conference or talk on the phone, and if the interview loop progressed to the point that they wanted to meet in person, I'd book a flight home. I decided to take the extended trip. With no overhead—no mortgage, utilities, no cable—and traveling as frugally as possible, and imposing on friends, I could make sure my meager unemployment, which capped out at six months, would be enough to travel the world while looking for a job.

JUST PIVOT

This plan felt right to me. It resonated with the sense of purpose I'd had all my life—to experience the world. I whittled my U.S. overhead to almost zero. I put my stuff in a storage locker, a deal where I paid one dollar a month for six months; disconnected my landline and cable; and stopped my car insurance. I turned the disruption of my personal life, the loss of my home and job, into freedom to travel. Sure, taking off could be seen as running away from my problems, but at the same time, I was saying there wasn't really a problem at all.

When you completely pivot in a different direction, you take yourself outside of your environment, which can be energizing and healing. If I stayed in Silicon Valley, everywhere I went I'd be faced with (what felt like) the ruins of my life. If I went out with friends, everyone would be talking about their amazing jobs, the fund-raising they'd done, their partners and families. I'd have nothing to contribute, which would make my circumstances even more painful. Plus, having sold my house, I'd have to explain to people that I was living with friends because I didn't have a job and couldn't afford to pay rent, let alone buy a new house, until I sorted out my situation. I just wasn't up for that.

But if I was traveling, I'd have time to regroup, away from painful reminders of my circumstances. No one would have any idea what my living situation was. They'd only know what I reported on social media. They'd check out Facebook, Twitter, Instagram to see what I was doing and think, *Wow, Gopi's in Iceland today.* Or *He's at some ashram in Rishikesh.*

So I wanted to dramatically and positively change my environment—which you can do too, on a small or large scale, if your circumstances permit. The large scale might be packing up and traveling, moving across the country, and at the risk of sounding trite, the small could be as simple as switching up your schedule. If you run, take a different route, or reverse your route. If you don't run, you could start. Turn on music and dance, just in your living room. Take a class. Walk around a part of the city you don't usually visit or spend a few hours in a neighboring town. Pop into a store you'd never go in—an antique store, jewelry store, retro clothing shop—just wander and be curious. Close your eyes and meditate.

Part of happiness is to not dwell too much on the past. You don't hide from it, but when it's traumatic or painful you rewrite it, rise above it, grow. So you're no longer walking around your old neighborhood in Palo Alto (let's just say) with everything you see reminding you of this life you no longer have. You can't block it out forever. There are many ways to deal, of course. This was the option that most appealed to me.

So, at 11 at night, warmed by the bright sun—because it's summer in Iceland and the sun never sets—you're walking down the amazing, moody, wild, and unpredictable Hekla volcano, which threatens to spew lava and ash sometime in the next 300 years. Who knows? But spew it will. Until then, it sits brooding and scowling, hissing gas that rises from deep inside the bowels of the earth, which boil with some unexpressed anger no one quite understands.

I had the trip of a lifetime in Iceland. Pamrod and his wife, Aroma, who were also from Kerala, indulged me by driving full circle around the island over a few days. Their hospitality for a complete stranger left me very touched. Their Icelandic friends, in turn, extended their hospitality by inviting us to stay in their homes, summer houses, farms, and guest rooms. Pramod and Aroma's precious five-year-old, Vibhu, was a delight, asking intelligent questions and telling jokes in three languages—English, Malayalam, and Icelandic. By the end of my trip, I was chanting nursery rhymes in Icelandic: *"Ullen, Thullen, Thol, Pike, Pane, Gol . . ."*

After Iceland, I took off for India to stay with my family. While there, I tweaked my travel model for the next few months (which I adhered to). I would be as careful with my money as possible; book the cheapest flights, all midweek, often with stopovers rather than direct; eat at roadside stands. And adhere to one hard-and-fast rule: no hotels. Instead, I'd already picked destinations where I knew someone. I planned to stay with friends I saw often and friends from high school whom I hadn't seen for years, friends who'd taken jobs in countries other than India, including Zambia, Bahrain, Sri Lanka.

I traveled around India, meeting friends from high school, college, engineering school; seeing my sisters and their families. Then I hopped over to Kenya, where my friend Manpreet had just been appointed deputy ambassador. Part of my go-to plan for global travel was to go wherever Manpreet was posted. Right now, he's in Afghanistan. I probably won't visit him there. But I did visit him many times when he was stationed in Peru and Mongolia.

During that trip following Iceland, my itinerary was determined by a simple formula: Whom do I know in country X that I haven't pissed off yet and will kindly give me room and board for a few days before his wife says to him, "I know you guys went to high school and all that, but when is that annoying guy leaving?" More than once, I heard my friends negotiating a few days for me by saying variations on "But he's sad."

KEEP TRYING

I broke my rule only once, when Manpreet and I traveled to climb Kilimanjaro. I didn't have any friends who lived at the bottom of the mountain, so the day before we started our climb, we stayed in a hotel. We traveled to Tanzania from Nairobi on a gently swaying but aggressively driven matatu minibus, the quintessential Kenyan people mover. Kilimanjaro loomed in the distance, its permanent snow cover a startling sight just a few hundred miles south of the equator. The mountain rises dramatically from the surrounding northern Tanzanian plains, alone in pancake-flat territory. At 19,340 feet, it is the tallest mountain in Africa and 5,000 feet higher than the tallest peak in the contiguous United States, Mount Whitney. It's also the tallest mountain in the world where one can hike all the way to the summit without technical climbing gear. That's part of the lure of Kilimanjaro, why so many people attempt it. Even though for the most part, it's an easy climb, it can still be challenging.

I was in awe, and because of that, I made two huge mistakes. First, I ignored the fact that I wasn't feeling well. I'd caught a bug somewhere during the previous two weeks in Africa. I felt terribly sick. I was in no position to go for a walk, let alone climb Africa's tallest mountain. The hotel staff took one look at me and bundled me, and my ineffective antibiotics, off to Kilimanjaro hospital, where Dr. Moro, a Russian-trained Tanzanian doctor, peered at me critically over the rim of his reading glasses.

"So, you're telling me that you've been taking these antibiotics for five days and you're still not feeling better." I fidgeted, looked down at my feet sheepishly, and apologized for my lack of physiological response to this pharmacological intervention. Dr. Moro said it could be a virus, in which case antibiotics wouldn't help, but he suspected I could have picked up a tropical parasite and sent me for a blood test. After a short time in the waiting room, Dr. Moro called me in to give the good news—no parasites—and the bad news: I should reconsider going up the mountain.

"Kilimanjaro is no joke," he lectured sternly. "There are no doctors up there. The evacuation methods for emergencies are extremely primitive, and the porters bringing you down aren't really concerned about providing the most comfortable ride for the patient." My head full of visions of being dropped into a gorge and the porters continuing on without realizing I was gone, I returned to the hotel. I spoke with Manpreet and our guide, and we decided we'd make a final decision the next morning.

The next morning, I felt slightly better, and one of the guides said, "We'll take it day by day. Each day we'll try it, and if you feel bad, we'll bring you back down to base camp." I nodded.

The second mistake I made was not giving myself enough time to acclimatize. There are seven routes you can take up Kilimanjaro. We chose the Marangu, or Coca-Cola, route, partly because it has trekkers' huts at all the camps and partly because it is the most popular of all the routes. You can make the trek in five days—three days up and two down—which is extremely hard on your body because you don't have a chance to acclimatize. Climbers who take five days have a 27 percent chance of reaching Uhuru Peak, the highest point in all of Africa. If you make it, you've summited.

Or you can take seven days—five days up and two days down, which is nice and gentle (or at least nicer and gentler) and gives your body more time to adapt. You stop along the way, set up camp, get your body settled, and then continue on, stop again, and so on up the mountain. Climbers who take seven days have a 92 percent chance of getting to the top.

Unfortunately, we signed up to take the five-day trek because Manpreet had to be at a U.N.-related conference. These two elements—being sick and not taking the time to acclimatize—made the trip a bit tougher for me.

The first day, our group of nine set out from Marangu Gate, elevation 6,036. We walked through a dense rain forest to our camp at 9,000 feet. The second day, we climbed to 12,000 feet. The first half of that walk was agonizingly steep, but sheer determination kept me going. The third day, we walked for six hours across the saddle between Kibo and Mawenzi Peaks before climbing again through a steeper and rougher path at Jiwe La Ukoyo. The walk across the saddle was desolate and reminded me of the red rocks of Utah. Monotony and drudgery are your biggest enemy when you're climbing, so I tried to be present in the moment and observe the Alpine desert vegetation—cactus, thorn bushes, groundsel, lobelia, oleander. It was a slow, steady climb, agonizing at that altitude, with the thin air supplying not nearly enough oxygen.

I'd been warned against the dangers of not acclimatizing well. Your body can behave strangely. Your head aches. You feel nauseated, become disoriented, and in the worst-case scenario—what kills mountaineers, especially novices—you can suffer from pulmonary or cerebral edema, where, because of the low pressure, your lungs and/or brain expand beyond a healthy point, fill with fluid, and rupture. So there was all that floating in my head. Twice we saw stretchers coming down with a climber bundled in a sleeping bag, lying still. At first I thought the climbers were dead, but I was told they were suffering from altitude sickness. Again came the visions of exploding heads and burst lungs.

Finally, at about 4 P.M., we arrived at the final camp of Kibo, at 15,500 feet. In a forbidding lunar landscape of rock and shale, Kibo lay at the bottom of the 4,000-foot vertical cone that is the crater of the Kilimanjaro summit. Just looking up at the summit made us giddy. We all tried not to think of the final climb to come shortly because we were sure that if we dwelled on it, we'd turn away and descend. The cooks made us a warm meal to fuel us for the final assault. One whiff of the stew and I dragged myself outside the hut, threw up, then hauled myself back in to try to ingest some of it. But I couldn't eat. No one could. We were too nervous thinking of the task ahead. We went to bed and tried to sleep for a few hours before we were roused at 11 P.M. so we could start the final climb at midnight. At that hour, the volcanic sand slopes leading to the summit would be frozen, and you'd slide down less.

I didn't sleep well. I had developed a headache, a tight metal band squeezing my head. I was sure I was experiencing one of the classic but mild signs of high-altitude cerebral edema. Brad Reinke, an expedition doctor who accompanied all the Wharton leadership programs to high altitudes and had climbed with me on the lower slopes of Kanchenjunga in the Himalayas a few years before, had e-mailed me earlier with some instructions. One was that if I woke up with a headache, I shouldn't go any higher. I lay in my bed thinking *I shouldn't do this*, but I nodded off, and when I was roused at 11, my headache was gone. Unsure whether I'd imagined it all, beaten it, or was deceiving myself into thinking I was fine, I decided to get dressed and go.

The goal was to get to the top before sunrise. I didn't make it. The air was thin and freezing. My breath was labored, my gait unbearably slow. One step. Pause. Another step. Pause. One hour in, maybe two, I realized I was falling behind as the rest of the group broke away. I heard one of our guides, Benny, say to another, *"Polé, polé."* Something to the effect that I was going very slowly. Gabriel, the head guide, came back down to talk to me. "I'm definitely beginning to feel the effects of the high altitude," I said. "This is as fast as I can go." It was a long way up to the summit and things weren't going to get easier, so he advised me to turn back to camp. I wished the rest of the group good luck and started descending slowly, almost with a sense of relief.

Gabriel walked back with me, supporting me. I felt dizzy, out of it. "Lie down on your bed and get some rest," he said. "If you feel any worse, come get me." Then he left, locking me in the hut by mistake. Shortly afterward, I felt like I needed to go out and throw up, but I was trapped. I pounded on the wooden walls, but nobody heard me. All the climbers and guides were on the mountain. The porters were in their tents out of earshot. I felt quite stupid. There are many heroic ways to die on an expedition, but this would be the silliest. My epitaph would read, "He choked on his puke trapped in a climbers' hut." Finally, one of our group, who'd returned with a guide after I had, heard my banging and let me out. I threw up, then returned to the hut and lay there. It was a few hours before I was able to get up and move around.

Later, as we descended the mountain, we were all silent, reflecting on our personal experiences. Those who'd reached the summit felt an incredible sense of accomplishment along with a resolve never to make the climb again. It was simply too physically demanding. Those who turned back at various points before summiting were haunted by ghosts. Had they given up too quickly? Should they have tried to ascend over five days instead of three? Should they have taken Diamox to stave off altitude sickness?

One woman was particularly unforgiving of herself. She told every climber we passed who would listen that she'd almost reached the summit and regretted having to turn back. I asked Gabriel at least three times if I'd turned back too soon. He assured me I'd made a wise decision. He says it would have been easy to evacuate me from Kibo, but if I'd gone on and been closer to the summit when things went wrong, I could have died.

When I stopped second-guessing myself, I realized that I'd learned something important. It didn't matter whether I'd summited. I'd pushed myself. I'd tested the boundaries (which may have not been very smart in my condition, but still). You never know how far you can go until you try. Making the attempt, seeing what I was capable of even in the worst conditions, gave me the confidence that I could try again. Summiting is a great experience, and you can have bragging rights, but ultimately, you're really competing against yourself and any sense of limitations that you may have.

Sir Edmund Hillary said, "It's not the mountain we conquer, but ourselves." While I didn't completely conquer myself—and what does that mean anyway?—I did explore inner and outer terrain, expand, stretch to the utmost of my capabilities at the time. Kim Moriyama, an Outward Bound instructor who guided my group up Mount Galena in Colorado several years ago, told us at the summit that "mountains don't know how high they are. They just sit there. You have to respect them and climb them slow and steady. And if you don't make it, you can always come back. Mountains have been sitting there for five million years. They will be there another year waiting for you."

Okay, so none of us have five million years to get it right, but the idea is, we can try again. And while unlike a mountain, the same opportunity might not offer itself in the same way, our ultimate destination will be there.

BE SPECIFIC ABOUT WHAT YOU WANT

As important as it is to take flying leaps into the unknown, it's also important to ground yourself. While I was traveling, I knew I needed to find an anchor. So, especially when I was traveling through India after circling Iceland, I sought out monasteries and ashrams and spent time there. At Rama Shakti Mission in Mangalore, I set the intention to find the ideal job. I wrote down the kind of companies I wanted to work for and then got more specific. I drew on the wise words I'd read in Richard Bolles's

What Color Is Your Parachute? He said essentially that when you're doing a job search, the more focused you are, the more likely you'll get the kind of job you're most interested in. He said to be very, very specific about the companies and opportunities you want to go after.

It makes sense. If you tell people you specifically want to work for Microsoft, AT&T, or Amazon in product development as a systems development manager, then people can help you. This level of specificity is diametrically opposed to the usual request I get: "I'm looking for something interesting in Silicon Valley. Do you know of any opportunities?" You can barely help anyone with that type of vague request. So, drawing on Bolles's advice, I came up with a list of companies I wanted to work for: Google, Yahoo, and SAP. Just three. After Kilimanjaro, I stayed with Manpreet in Nairobi for a few days. When I finally checked my in-box, I had an e-mail from a headhunter, saying SAP wanted to interview me. I didn't even know how they knew I was looking for a job.

I sent an e-mail to SAP and said I was in Kenya, so I set up my first interview by phone from there. Our next interview call was from Bahrain. The third and final call was with the hiring manager; I had that call when I was back in India. And then Yahoo contacted me. It was time to go home.

My friend Sukumar picked me up at the San Francisco airport. Forgetting that I was returning from a long trip and would have a lot of baggage, he drove up in his two-seater Miata convertible. There was no place to put my stuff. I ended up sitting in the passenger seat, top down, seat belt strapped, while my friend piled my bags and everything else I'd brought back on top of me. He kept laughing at how he'd completely forgotten I was returning from a long trip. "Welcome to America," he said. It was the same thing my friend Rakesh had said to me years earlier when I'd flown in from Singapore and he'd set me up at the Berkeley YMCA, where I sat in a chair at the end of the hall dropping coins into the pay phone, cold-calling companies I wanted to work for to set up interviews.

"Welcome to America," Sukumar said again, then hopped in the car and sped off down the freeway, with me clutching my bags and who knows what else. When we got to his house, I turned on my phone for the first time in six months (they didn't work internationally then). Three minutes later it rang. The headhunter from Google wanted to talk to me. I'd applied at Google months earlier through a classmate from Wharton who worked there, so it wasn't totally out of the blue, but the timing of it all was marvelous. Here I was after six months of not really focusing on my professional career and my target companies were all engaging with me. No other companies. Just those three. There was something a bit mystical around it all.

I also had a message from SAP; they'd scheduled my final round of interviews the day I was having surgery on my hand, something I'd put off forever. They agreed to push everything back to the next day, and I went on that series of interviews with my hand in a sling, my ears ringing and stomach burning from too many aspirin to cut the pain. During interviews, I tend to get up from my chair and draw on a whiteboard to make my point. In this case I could barely write, because I had to use my nondominant hand. But I didn't let any of that faze me. I wrote anyway. Somehow I managed to navigate my way through the interviews and was offered the job.

During that same period, I went through a round of interviews with Google for two positions, neither of which quite worked, so I bagged that idea and thought, *Okay, I'll join SAP.* Which I did. Months later Google came back and said, "In the last few interviews, the people who talked to you were quite impressed, but they weren't quite sure what the best fit would be, so we sort of kept you in a floating state. Now we've found a great opportunity for you. Could you please come back and talk to us?" So I did, and this time they asked me about a role that I'd not even imagined I'd be the best candidate for. But that's the nice thing about the recruiting process at Google. They spot talent and figure out what might be the best way to utilize that talent, which is pretty impressive.

I started as director of strategic marketing with Google's AdSense and then with AdWords. I'd never even considered a career in marketing, but I was happy to do just about anything at Google. That was another piece of advice Richard Bolles gives in his book: To find your dream job in a company, find *a* job at the company because once you're inside, you can weave magic with that social capital. I'm still there today, and the job I have now is incredibly satisfying and delightful.

Who knows, if I hadn't taken that trip, I might never have written down those three companies. I might never have interviewed twice at Google, thinking I'd failed only to be called back months later for a job I'd never thought of pursuing in a field I otherwise wouldn't have realized I loved. I definitely wouldn't have stumbled down the mountain to base camp, my brains threatening to blow out my ears, arming myself with experience for future climbs up a wise mountain going nowhere.

Next time you're feeling shattered or stuck or you're having a bad day (or a great one), shake things up. Trust your heart. Pivot toward what resonates. Pivot again. And prepare for something mystical.

D🙂N'T FAIL, MORPH

It is impossible to live without failing at something, unless you live so cautiously that you might as well not have lived at all. In which case, you fail by default.

— J. K. Rowling

You know what it feels like to come back from vacation. You've had fun, relaxed, opened yourself to a new environment, new people, new experiences. Each time away changes you a bit. Something shifts. You come back and say to yourself, *I'm going to hold on to that feeling.* But how do you do that? How do you lock that shift in, continue to keep morphing toward your highest potential?

When I returned from Iceland, I felt grounded, peaceful, slipping back into my largely optimistic self. Flipping my temporarily tragic (to me) circumstances into an opportunity to explore the world helped me get to that place inside. I wanted to hold on to that feeling.

I've found that mixing things up, keeping things new, shifting, changing, while always keeping true to myself, helps me expand, feel centered and, well, happy. I had the part about keeping things new covered. I was relatively newly single, which still didn't feel so great, but I had a new job I was excited about and a new a condo I loved. No

101

more couch surfing around the globe, my friends' spouses barely tolerating me and, after a few days, hard-selling the delights of the next country over.

But while I felt largely invigorated that I'd made it almost to the top of Mount Kilimanjaro (before I had to turn around and slink off back to base camp in the dead of night), a bit of a loser element persisted. Then I saw an ad for the Super Sprint TRI for FUN, and that element began to dissipate. Triathlons consist of swimming, biking, and running, in that order—one race immediately following another. Distances vary. But just so you can see where the race that caught my notice stacked up in the hierarchy, here are the distances for different types of triathlons.

- Sprint: Swim 0.5 miles, bike 12.4 miles, run 3.1 miles.

- Olympic: Swim 0.93 miles, bike 24.8 miles, run 6.2 miles.

- ITU long: Swim 1.86 miles, bike 49.6 miles, run 12.4 miles.

- Half Ironman: Swim 1.2 miles, bike 56 miles, run 13.1 miles.

- Ironman: Swim 2.4 miles, bike 112 miles, run 26.2 miles.

Then there was the Super Sprint TRI for FUN: Swim 400 yards, bike 12 miles, and run 3.1 miles. It seemed possibly doable, a way to build my confidence. *Why not?* I thought. *What can I lose by trying?* So I signed up. No idea what I was doing. No training. I decided the Silicon Valley Triathlon Club could wait; training could wait. I was determined. My goal wasn't to win; it was to cross the finish line.

Plus, with all that had gone down six months before, entering a triathlon was my way of taking revenge. Not in the way the expression is usually used when you feel wronged and want to get back at someone by spiting them or acting as badly as they did. No, I meant revenge in the sense that "the best revenge is a life well lived." Revenge against whatever life throws your way—spinning it on its axis.

NOT AT ALL FUN

As the race grew nearer, I began to think about logistics. I could bike. I could run. No problems there. But swimming, that had me a little worried. I'd never swum outside a pool, where I could manage laps, and if I felt tired I could swim to the side and grab on to the edge or go to the shallow end and stand up. When I was growing up in Kerala, there were 30 million people in the state, and the number of swimming pools in the entire state, at that time, was one. Okay, so no great swimmers from Kerala. I learned how to swim, sort of, but I was never really comfortable outside a pool where I couldn't touch the bottom or hold on to something. So I practiced a bit for swimming, but foolishly, only in a pool, never in open water.

The morning of the triathlon, I got up before sunrise, dragged my commuter bike out of the garage and strapped it to my bike rack, stowed my gear—bike helmet, swim cap, water bottles, GU energy packets—in the back seat of my Prius, and took off on 680 East for the 45-minute trip across San Francisco Bay to Shadow Cliffs park. I was in danger of losing my breakfast, but I kept my eyes on the road, focused on my breathing, and began to calm down a bit. *What's the worst that can happen?* As always, once I figured that out, taking the risk was much easier. I wasn't going to drown. There were lifeguards. Even if I bombed, didn't make it to the finish line, I'd have bombed with pride. I'd have changed. I'd have learned something. I'd know more. It's funny, don't you think, how fear can get in our way, but if we just go for it, no matter what happens, we feel a sense of possibility because we leaned in.

When I got to the park, I unpacked and made my way to the lake for the swimming portion of the race. Thousands of people in suits and swim caps, along with friends, families, and supporters, clogged the beach. Triathletes commiserating, pacing, waiting to hit the lake, a former quarry surrounded by sun-scorched hills and scrub oak. We had to swim out, around two buoys, and back—400 yards total. I stared at the water, the buoy, the mass of humanity around me. So many swimmers waiting to crash into the lakeweed-infested waters. Too many.

Where are the lifeguards? I looked around the beach. Thank god. They were everywhere, 20 or 30 of them. They knew how to work this event. They'd been working these triathlons for years. I spotted one close by—legs wide, arms crossed, alert, gazing at the lake through his polarized Costas. I made my way toward him, leaving a trail of footprints behind me, possibly close to the last I'd ever leave.

I introduced myself and shook his hand. "I'm not sure how I'll do in the water," I said. "Please keep an eye on me." I tried to keep my tone serious but short of pleading. "I'm in the last wave." That's what they called the groups we were divided into.

"Thanks for letting me know," he said. "We'll be watching, and if you get in trouble, wave your hands."

"Okay, but how will you see me?"

"We obviously can't keep a close eye on thousands of people—"

My stomach flipped. *Is he kidding?*

"—but we have a system. We know who to watch extremely closely. There are always a few in each wave. We'll watch out for you."

"Okay." I nodded. *Okay.* I walked a few feet away and turned toward the water. They called the first wave. A huge group of triathletes lined up by the shore, adjusting their caps, waving their arms to loosen up. While they tried to look casual, the air hummed with panic. Or maybe the panic was all mine. I didn't know. I couldn't think straight. *Breathe. Hold.*

I jumped when the horn blasted. The first wave rushed to the water. My focus intense, I watched for any keys to success I might pick up at the last minute. You could tell the level of expertise in each wave. Strong swimmers just dove in—a surface-skimming racing dive. They miraculously stayed on top of the water, cutting through it, homing in on the buoy. The next level of swimmers ran into the water until it was deep enough to swim and took off. The slower or more unsure swimmers walked into the water, as they would in a pool. These were my people. These were also the people at risk. With each wave of swimmers, the lifeguards pulled two or three of the less experienced from the lake.

Finally they called my wave. The horn blared, and I took off, feet dragging, toward the water, into the water, sinking into the clay-rich bottom, making my way as best I could. I knew I wasn't going to win. I'd also lowered my goal from crossing the finish line to just not dying. So why struggle? Waist-deep now. The tangled forest of lakeweed grabbing my legs, sliming my stomach, as I waded through the murky, churned-up water. In a pool you can see bottom. Not here. I had no business being in this lake. The unsure swimmers ahead of me—okay, close to every single one of the walkers—started to swim. Someone slapped me in the face, another kicked me. Flying arms and legs everywhere. My throat tightened. I felt as though I were in a scene from Alfred Hitchcock's *The Birds*, swarmed by an airborne stampede of wing-flapping crows. *No problem.* I told myself. *It's a short distance. Just swim out, touch the buoy, and swim back.*

It's okay, I chanted in my mind (or very possibly out loud). *It's okay. I'm going to be okay.* The water was up to my chin. *I'm going to be okay.* My lower lip. Any second now I'd have to start swimming. I lifted off, clawed at the water. What had I been thinking? I had zero experience swimming in any body of water other than a pool. This was no pool. I couldn't see bottom. Was there a bottom? This was open water. I was out of my league. I started sinking, swallowed water. Swallowed more. I was drowning. *Stay calm!* I waved my hands. *They'll be here quickly.* And *I've got to get through this.* Then, *Gosh, I've got a dinner party at my house tonight.* And until the guards got there, that thought was uppermost in my mind. It's funny how, in what might be your last moments of life, such profound thoughts come to you.

Within seconds, two lifeguards were there with a surfboard. They made me hang on to the board. "Race is over for you," the one with the visor said. Hanging on to the surfboard, I felt a little safer.

"Can you guys stay with me?" I asked as I kicked. "I'll keep swimming and you just stay on my left and my right." My plan B. I could make this work.

"No way," the other guy said. "Once you start to drown, signal for help, it's over. You can go do the rest of the stuff if you want—get on your bike, run, but no swimming."

They pulled up next to a motorboat, lifted me on, and left. One of the lifeguards in the boat checked me out, made sure I was okay; then they took me back to shore. I climbed out of the boat and walked toward the crowd sitting on the shore who'd come to cheer on the swimmers, soak up the drama. They were clapping. For me. Cheering. *I'm disqualified. So why are they cheering?*

I was told later that it was in support: "Don't worry; at least you tried." But my own theory is that they cheered because they had nothing else to do. It wasn't like they could applaud the swimmers. They couldn't even see who was in the lead or lagging behind. It was a big thrashing blur. More along the lines of "This guy came back; we might as well applaud." I think they applauded out of boredom, but I could be wrong.

I smiled, waved at a few, and headed for the transition area to biking. I wasn't going home yet. I'd gotten up early, hauled my bike—I wasn't going to leave after two minutes in the water. So I trudged through the crowd, my mind off waving my arms and ruined dinner parties, my focus on the next race.

BIKING SETBACK #1

I finished the road bike ride and dirt trail run with no problem, and driving home, oddly, I discovered I was high on having gone through with it—happy and hooked. I wanted to enter another race, to cross the finish line. But first I needed to train. Training would help me to exact my revenge, keep me healthy, vigorous, outdoors. It was

THE HAPPY HUMAN

already July, midway through the season, but I decided to go to the triathlon club training sessions anyway. I took open-water swimming lessons with one of the coaches. And signed up to start running and biking with the group. The people at the club were amazing. Some men, but predominantly women—all active, athletic, fit. They were pretty aggressive, type A, but they competed with themselves, not one another. Their energy was uplifting, supportive. I was super motivated about getting up at 6:30 A.M. on the weekends and training with them.

The first time I went out, I pulled my commuter bike out of the garage, strapped it to my bike rack, and headed out to meet with the group. I was so green. I didn't even take a pump. I didn't know you had to regularly fill your tires. When I arrived, I'm sure it was painfully clear I was a newbie, but no one rolled their eyes at my commuter bike. They just welcomed me to the group.

We started off on a back road. Immediately it became clear that I wouldn't be able to keep pace with the rest of the group. They'd all started training together at the beginning of the season and had a regular sequence and cadence they'd built up to. I kept struggling to keep pace. Suddenly I was pushing harder and gaining less ground. I had a flat tire. I completely dropped out, and the coach, Mike, had to hang back with me to fix my tire. He explained that the club's program was a long-established one. Many of the members had been training for years. He strongly suggested I wait until the next season to start training. "Start at the beginning of the season with a new group," he said, then sent me home via a different route.

"I'll be back," I told him, sounding as upbeat as I could. "Next season." Then I hopped on my bike and rode off. I felt terrible. My athletic endeavors were doing nothing for my already dinged confidence. I'd had to bail on Mount Kilimanjaro, had nearly drowned during my micro triathlon, and now I'd been drummed out of this extremely supportive group. I needed to adjust my attitude, to see these defeats as stepping-stones (to who knew where), opportunities (for what I didn't know). I just knew it felt right to continue. So I decided to go on faith. Trust the universe. I continued my swimming lessons, ran, kept up with my yoga practice, and the next season, I bought a shiny new triathlon bike and started training with the group. But the universe, which allegedly had my back, wasn't done throwing curveballs. *Trust,* I told myself. *Go with what feels right.* I plodded on.

BIKING SETBACK #2

The next setback came partway through the training season, when the group and I were winding our way down a side street in Palo Alto. I hit something in the road, braked, and in what felt like slow motion, flipped spectacularly over the handlebars. There I was, flat on my back, wondering, *What just happened?* Then, *Why don't they put seat belts on bicycles?* The team stopped. The coach stopped. No one could figure out what had happened. There was nothing in the road. It was just like when you trip and fall for no obvious reason when you're walking on a flat surface. I got up, dusted myself off. My bike was only slightly bent. I had only minor bruises. But the fall definitely rattled me and affected my training.

Discouraged, ready to quit but not wanting to, I dragged myself to the new-member orientation at the triathlon club that night. The speaker, Jayne Williams, stood on the stage. By no stretch of the imagination did

THE HAPPY HUMAN

she look like a lean, hungry fighting machine of muscle. She started by saying, "I'm a triathlete too." She'd just finished writing her book *Slow Fat Triathlete: Live Your Athletic Dreams in the Body You Have Now*. Whatever stereotype or image you may have of a triathlete, she took it head-on. The woman sitting to my left leaned over and said, "Isn't she great? If you're enjoying her mold-busting speech, you should read about Sister Madonna, a triathlete known as the Iron Nun."

I thanked her, and when I got home I googled Sister Madonna. She's a nun from Spokane, Washington, in her mid-70s at the time. She'd finished 300 triathlons, including 32 Ironmans. She started when a priest urged her to, saying it was "an excellent way to tweak mind, body, and spirit." When I read that sentence, I thought, *Maybe it was for her, but it's not looking good for my mind and my body.* Next, I found that she'd competed in her first triathlon when she was in her early 50s. Then she was my inspiration. I thought, *Wow. This woman could pick it up at 52 and do it. I'm in my 30s. I should be able to give it a go.*

YET ANOTHER BIKING SETBACK

After four months of training with the club, I was racing in my first triathlon. Seasoned triathletes haul their bikes in expensive trailers or mount them on a rack that locks them in, rock-solid. I had an old-fashioned rack that you mount on the trunk. They drove SUVs. I drove a compact passenger car. I worried about my bike rack each time I took my bike out. As I drove to the race, I glanced in the rearview mirror from time to time to make sure my bike was secure. At one point, I heard a kind of shuddering, but I was lost in a fog thinking about my time and the race.

A few miles later, I glanced up at the rearview mirror. No bike. The straps had come undone. I glanced in the mirror again. There I was, speeding away, while my bike bounced along behind me. Cars behind me swerved, jumped into another lane. Brakes screeched. A Mad Max demolition derby unfolding in my rearview mirror—all caused by me and my property. My stomach dropped. I was horrified.

Finally, what was left of my bike bounced and came to a rest in the middle of the right lane. I pulled over to the side of the road and just sat there, mortified. Some guy on his motorcycle slowed down, stopped, and yelled, "You almost killed me. Your bike fell in front of me, and I had to swerve in front of another car that almost smashed into me." I apologized, kept apologizing. He calmed down, merged with traffic, and took off. Meanwhile, the cars around me were slowly passing.

Within five minutes, a cop arrived. I opened my door. "Stay in your car," he said. "It's too dangerous out here. Property is replaceable. Life is not." He tore gnarled pieces of my bike from my car, set them on the side of the road, then picked up the rest of my bike from where it had come to rest in the right lane and dumped it on top of the smashed pieces. He came up to my car and told me to go home. He'd take care of removing the disaster that was my bike. I looked at the pile of titanium, the cost almost equal to a month's mortgage. It felt like a foreclosure.

MAKING LEMONADE

I bought a new bike, but I didn't compete in any triathlons that year. I was a bit fearful after all my setbacks. What would happen next? But I had a deep desire to continue, so I trusted that desire and kept training, and the next year, after hundreds of painful miles on the road and in the water, I completed my first triathlon, a Super Sprint TRI for FUN. Seven hours after racing toward the water, I was almost the last person to limp across the finish line. After that I started competing more and more. I got better. My performance was nothing outstanding, but I knocked my time down to about two and a half hours. A seasoned triathlete could go through the entire course in 45, 50 minutes, but I didn't care. I was thrilled. I still compete in the Super Sprint TRI for FUN every couple of years to keep my hand in. For me, it's still daunting, but I enjoy it.

Between that first triathlon I completed and my near drowning nearly two years earlier, I didn't compete in a single triathlon. Not one. But all that training, all those setbacks, fueled a different win. I gave a speech about those initial efforts, and that speech took me to the semi-finals of the Toastmasters International World Championship of Public Speaking. Now I often tell people that I was a failed triathlete but became a successful public speaker on the shoulders of that failure.

About the time I completed my first triathlon, I was interviewed by a researcher who was writing a book about resilience. "This is just pretty incredible," he said when he heard about what I'd done during the past two years. "Normally, when people have some sort of crisis in their lives, it takes a long while for them to bounce back. They're not racing off and doing triathlons and going to Iceland and climbing Kilimanjaro right away." I just shrugged, hands open to the heavens. To me, it felt like the most natural thing in the world to do—to keep going, veering left at normal, trying something new. It didn't matter that I turned back from the peak of Kilimanjaro. It was okay that I'd been hauled out of the water. The joy, the freedom, was that I'd tried something new. Taken risks.

You don't have to take crazy Alex Honnold–style risks. (Actually, I don't know of anyone who takes that scale risk.) Alex is the world's greatest free-solo mountain climber, who scaled the 3,000-foot vertical face of Yosemite's El Capitan without a harness or rope. Just him and the granite wall. "I was pretty much elated," he told The Associated Press about reaching the top of the mountain. "I was probably the happiest I've ever been. It's something that I thought about for so long and dreamed about and worked so hard for. I mean, it's pretty satisfying." Taking risks, stepping out of our box, setting new goals and going for them, works like that. It makes us happy. Think about the day you ditched your training wheels and, after a few tries, went solo, sailed off down the street. Yeah. A whole new world. Remember that feeling?

Think about it. What have you had a secret desire to do? How can you shake things up, to keep contentment and purpose and joy in your life? Set a goal. Challenge yourself. Take the first step, then another. Just follow your heart, and start tripping along.

EXPECT
MIRACLES

To me every hour of the light and dark is a miracle. Every cubic inch of space is a miracle.

— WALT WHITMAN

Every day, I wake up and say out loud, "I expect a miracle in my life today." Every single day I put that message out to the universe. I started this practice after listening to a friend, the author Gabby Bernstein, speak at Google. She talked about the transformational power of looking for and expecting a miracle each and every day of your life. My happiness comes from being aware and present to those miracles and celebrating each one. These miracles can be like bread crumbs, signaling that we're on the right course, or helping us course-correct. To me, they're reminders to heed Rumi's words, to "live life as though everything is rigged in your favor." They signal the possible, hope, something greater.

Most days, a miracle, either small or large, takes place. On the days it doesn't, I'm sure it's because I'm distracted, caught up in work, and I forget to look for or recognize the miracle.

These miracles can be very ordinary. They don't have to be a sea parting, someone walking on water, or a voice booming from the heavens. Every day, so many things happen in what is considered an ordinary life. Some small, some big—they're all miracles. I'm not talking about your being suddenly transformed, and in some mystical process you start manifesting miracles, and soon the world gathers at your doorstep, and a shrine is built for you, and a candle is lit at your statue. That's not what I'm saying. I'm taking a much more pedestrian view: that so much of our life is indeed a miracle, and you just have to open your eyes and be present to it.

Some days, I might find a miracle in the smallest thing—a text or call from a friend who's suddenly on my mind, or a parking space. Other days, that miracle is more a delightful surprise, which I count as a miracle. Sometimes that miracle is incredible on a global, mega-breathtaking scale, where seemingly out of nowhere an opportunity presents itself, a door opens. To me, these miracles, large and small, signal that some cosmic goings-on are at play. They signal possibility, which fills me with joy and inspires me to take chances—because I will land.

DELIGHTFUL SURPRISE

Let me give you an example of a miracle in the delightful surprise category. After two months of traveling on Saturdays and Sundays, I was home, sleeping snugly in my own bed, sipping home-brewed cups of clove-scented masala chai, delighting in the soothing sound of the waves lapping the dock outside my bedroom window. All week I'd been looking forward to going to the monthly Saturday night Non Stop Bhangra dance party in San Francisco. I hit the event whenever I can. In the nightclub, out on the dance floor, I shake off the workweek. Totally cutting loose, arms flying in a jerky, disjointed fashion, a star in my own Bollywood movie, surrounded by thumping feet and swirling colors—vivid reds, brilliant blues, light-bright yellows.

The day of the event, I always e-mail 10 or 12 friends to meet me there. But that Saturday, when I looked at my calendar, I realized I had the dates mixed up. It was the following weekend. There I was, a rare weekend in town, with nothing on my calendar—no agenda, no one to see. And nowhere to go. So I called my friend Stuart, hoping that we could meet for a drink, dinner, anything, but he had already made plans with a few of his friends to go roller-disco skating at a rink near my house. He asked me to join them. I hadn't skated in 20 years, but I figured *Why not?* and went along.

When we got to the rink, I stood inside the door, transported back to the 1970s. The Bee Gees blared from the speakers. Skaters decked out in crazy flared-sleeve, body-hugging, flashy-belted disco funk glided round and round the rink under a spinning mirrored ball. Excited/determined/resigned, I rented my skates. Then, hugging them to my chest, I made my way to the bleachers surrounding the rink, sat on a bench, kicked off my shoes—step one accomplished—and took in my surroundings.

So much going on. Sitting at the tables on the sidelines, revelers wearing ridiculous hats and blowing horns handed out squares of birthday cake. And on the rink, to the tunes of Sister Sledge, Kool & the Gang, and Village People, flamboyant skaters whizzed by at what felt like Mach speed, confident, graceful, high on the anachronistic joy of it all. I was in awe of them. I was also freaked out. Sighing, I bent down, wedged my feet into my skates, and laced up. Step two. Check. I started to get up, and sat right back down. It didn't look like there was going to be a step three. Did I mention I hadn't skated in 20 years? I just didn't have the confidence to go out skating on my own. So I sat there. Regrouping. Maybe it would be for the entire night.

After a few minutes, Stuart showed up, tapped me on the shoulder, and held out his hand. "I'll go around with you," he said.

I nodded to him. "Probably a good idea," I said. I scoped out the rink one more time and saw with relief that a few people were more at my level—three-, four-, and five-year-olds clutched their parents' hands as their moms or dads guided them slowly away from the rails, the kids gingerly stepping, not yet gliding, building their confidence. It was so sweet to watch. If those kids dared put wheels to wood, dwarfed by racing, spinning, jumping, pose-striking John Travolta and Donna Summer wannabes, I could too.

Stuart and I made our way onto the rink. There we were—step-sliding through the hotshots, brave kids, and a few teenagers shoving each other, yelling, not fazing anyone—clutching each other's hands, barely standing up. It was hilarious. Taking my eyes off my feet for a minute, I saw a woman in a group celebrating a birthday, pointing me out to the other moms. They couldn't stop laughing. I'm sure I looked fairly nervous. Stuart and I both must have looked silly. But who cared? I was staying upright and circling the rink. That was my miracle for that day. Going through a life experience I hadn't planned on, that I was hesitant about but did anyway, and it turned out to be fun and delightful. An unexpected opportunity to open up, get out of my head, risk. Thank you, Stuart.

Sometimes the delightful surprise can be on a grander scale. I had this experience during and immediately following the 2017 Wisdom 2.0 conference in San Francisco.

At the speakers' dinner, I got to know Jewel, the folk singer, and her manager and team. By a fluke, they'd all joined my friend Amandine and me at a remote table. I think we all needed a bit of quiet. There sat Jewel, a four-time Grammy Award nominee with an incredible story about experiencing life with wholeness and what it means to be a "farmer of light," a story she wrote about in her book *Never Broken*. I'd been completely moved by her speech and told her so. In *Never Broken*, she writes, "We cannot always control or avoid what happens to us, but we can control what it does to our spirit. And the quality of our spirit becomes the filter through which we see life." Human resilience is a miracle. Jewel's story certainly proves that.

During the dinner, I sat next to Jewel's manager, Marc Oswald. We discussed music, my own band Kirtan Lounge, the speeches at the conference, yoga, and Jewel's website, which is all about learning to make happiness a habit. As a thank-you for his time and attention, I gave Marc a copy of my book and our second Kirtan Lounge CD, *Precious Jewels*. A few days later, out of the blue, he called me. He told me he loved my book and had been listening to our Kirtan Lounge CD every day and thought it was beautiful. He said he'd spoken with Jewel about the album. "Is there something we can do with this?" he'd asked her. "Some way to help these guys?" As members of the Recording Academy, they could sponsor us for the Grammys. And with our okay, he said, they'd nominate us in five categories.

Wow. I could barely breathe. But there was no time for passing out. There was more.

"I want to bring you down to do an event with Jewel," he said to me, "a fund-raiser for her charity, Project Clean Water. Jewel will perform. Kirtan Lounge will perform.

You and Jewel will speak about your music; then you can teach yoga—an all-day event." Plus, to build buzz for the Grammys, he said he would invite members of the Recording Academy.

So all of that—from the dinner to the call—was a big, delightful surprise. I didn't wake up the day of the dinner thinking, *I'm going to sit next to the manager of one of the top folk singers in the world. He'll take a liking to me, my book, and our CD and will offer to help get our album into the Grammys.* But by some fluke, that's exactly what happened.

Months later, the event seems like a long shot (although we've scheduled it). And we weren't nominated for the Grammys, but still, to have even been sponsored. Amazing. And who knows? There's always next year. And the next. And . . .

GLOBAL MEGA-BREATHTAKING MIRACLE—HANGOUTS

A year after I returned from meeting His Holiness the Dalai Lama, the meeting I wrote about in the introduction to this book, his office expressed an interest in Google+, the product I was working on at the time. In *The Internet to the Inner-Net*, I wrote about this incident, how I started noodling around, scribbling down a few ideas. What if we got the Dalai Lama and his good friend Archbishop Desmond Tutu in a Google Hangout that we'd broadcast on the Internet to thousands, a million, who knew? I wrote it down as an intention, told a few people, and that was it. Five days later, I got a call at 1 A.M. from a colleague, Jonathan, in South Africa. The Dalai Lama was set to be the main guest at Desmond Tutu's birthday party, but he was having trouble with his visa. "The Arch has asked if we can use technology to find a solution," Jonathan said. A Hangout was the answer. We had 60 hours. A dozen Googlers in four countries swung into action. Seven days after I wrote down my intention, the Dalai Lama and Desmond Tutu, half a world apart, met on Google Hangouts. In just seven days, a crazy idea I wrote on a piece of paper transformed itself from intention to manifestation. That was a miracle. A global mega-breathtaking miracle.

A couple of days after Nelson Mandela died, I was asked to put together another Hangout for Desmond Tutu and the Dalai Lama to allow them time to share memories of their friend. It was to be three days after Archbishop Tutu delivered the eulogy in front of some 80,000 people. The Dalai Lama had confirmed, but until we got a yes from Archbishop Tutu, we couldn't move forward. Then, during one of the busiest weeks of his life, just two days before the event, he sent an e-mail (signed "Luv, Arch") saying he'd make it work. After that, through the effort of dozens of people, and with the help of just as many smaller miracles of timing and technology, the huge miracle we all expected came to be.

RECOGNIZING MIRACLES

Henry David Thoreau said, "All change is a miracle to contemplate; but it is a miracle which is taking place every second." When you think about it that way, change is a 24/7 stream of miracles, signals of possibility, signposts that the universe has got you covered. It's amazing. How can we not pay attention?

Really, we're just remembering how to spot miracles. For the most part, very young children don't separate miracles from their everyday existence. Miracles aren't miracles; they're simply the way things work. I've been trying to think of my first childhood miracle. One incident keeps coming to mind. One day, when I was very young, long before I studied yoga, I went into my parents' room. There I was, by myself, when suddenly, with no knowledge of what I was doing or why, I scrambled onto the bed, wound my legs into the lotus position, took a deep breath, and struck a yoga pose.

In a different era, people might say, "Oh, he must have seen that on YouTube or TV." But YouTube wasn't around yet, and we had no TV. No one in our town did. There was no broadcast station. Plus no one practiced yoga. There were no teachers, no studios. Who knew that what happened that day on my parents' bed would eventually lead me to this particular path and become so much a part of my life? Something guided me. I believe that. And that was a miracle.

If you look back, I'm sure you'll see patterns in your own life. And going forward, if you state your expectation for a miracle to occur each day, and watch for it, learn to recognize it, it will.

Miracles are everywhere. When you think about it, our entire lives are a miracle, if you look at the larger expansiveness of our world, one planet among nine in our one solar system, which is one among an estimated tens of billions in our galaxy. We're hurtling through space at 460 meters per second, spinning—and all the time, by some miracle, we're hanging on the globe, walking around, nobody falling off, not a hair out of place. A miracle.

Or what about the 2017 full solar eclipse? Everyone staring in awe at the sun through mass-produced solar-viewing glasses, DIY pinhole viewers, tricked-out Pringles cans. All because in some perfect, preordained order, the earth is spinning on its axis, circling the sun, and the moon is spinning on its axis, circling the earth. And every so often (every 375 years in the same place), the sun and moon come into perfect alignment, as on August 21, 2017. That eclipse, the biggest and best eclipse in American history cut a 70-mile-wide totality swath from Oregon to Georgia. But all the spinning, circling, aligning goes on each and every day. And while all this is going on, we continue our lives on this planet—cars zip to and from the office, the kids' school. Planes take off and land. Grass grows. Babies are born. One giant phenomenon. I didn't drive to Oregon to view the eclipse. But a lot of my friends went. They said it changed them. They said they stood in reverence, awe, and peace, looking on, pondering all that's so much bigger than we are. Witnessing a massive miracle.

I witnessed a major solar eclipse when I was a teenager, a prodigiously curious young person, eager to learn everything about anything. We didn't drive to the next state, as my friends did when they made the trek to the 60-mile "path of totality" in Oregon. When I was growing up in India, you didn't just pile in a car and hit the road to see an eclipse eight hours away. Long car trips were reserved for family gatherings and marriages and things like that, social structures or religious events. Or pilgrimages.

There was no need to leave town, though. A bunch of my friends and I heard that we could go to the local observatory and publicly participate. The place was filled with graduate students, physicists, astronomers, and other scientists—professionals working in the area—who explained the eclipse to us. I couldn't listen fast enough. We were getting so much information from these scientists in technical terms. The graduate students, my friends, and I were all asking questions, and the scientists had an explanation for pretty much everything we were seeing around us or were curious about. So, there was that thrill of witnessing this natural phenomenon *and* learning and being part of the process of scientific inquiry, which I was so caught up in. It was a lot like coming of age for me.

Why can't we keep that sense of awe every day? Like right now. We're balancing on this giant ball called Earth, part of a celestial dance, an amazing choreography. We sit here getting in a frenzy and arguing and talking and debating and marching and making funny sounds called music and dancing around a fire. Such awe-inspiring, astonishing wonder.

You don't have to drive to Oregon, because it's going on right now, all around you.

THE
P😊SSIBLEARIAN

I don't need easy, I just need possible.
— BETHANY HAMILTON, IN SOUL SEARCHER

I'm a possiblearian. I believe everything's possible. Possiblearians set a goal, put their minds to it, and somehow figure out a way to make it happen. That sense of potential creates so much joy and happiness because they're in a creative process, leveraging so many aspects of themselves. In Silicon Valley, "Nothing is impossible" is a mantra. Working at Google, known as one of the most innovative companies in the world, I see inventive problem solving every day. Google is all about possibility. In a society of possiblearians—and surrounding yourself with other possiblearians is key—you embrace the idea of infinite potential. No idea is too big, too out-there, too odd to be turned down.

AIM FOR 10X, NOT 10 PERCENT

Larry Page said in a *Wired* interview, "How exciting is it to come to work if the best you can do is trounce some other company who does roughly the same thing? That's why most companies decay slowly over time. They tend to do approximately what they did before with a few minor changes. It's natural for people to work on things they know aren't going to fail. But incremental improvement is guaranteed to become obsolete over time."

He was talking about the third principle in Google's Nine Principles of Innovation: Aim for 10x, which is about striving to improve something by a factor of 10 rather than just improving it by 10 percent. The idea of 10x is not exclusive to Google, but it's a big part of our culture. All our 10x solutions come from letting minds wander, going off and solving problems in crazy ways that don't yet exist, don't fit within any boundaries, don't seem possible. But they are.

A great example of 10x thinking occurred when a team in Google's X division—with "x" being the big problem that needs solving—saw that the Internet was unavailable to more than half the people in the world, mostly in rural or remote areas. "Okay," this person said, "why don't we take an Internet signal from the ground, beam it into the sky, and . . . let's say there's a giant transponder that reflects the Internet beam over a 100-mile radius and everyone living in that area will have access to Internet?" Right off the bat, you could say, "That's a completely ridiculous idea because there is no giant mirror in the sky." But this person and his team on the project were determined. "No, no. We *can* put a giant mirror in the sky." And now they're doing it. It's called Project Loon.

The idea is to rig a network of clear polyethylene wind- and solar-powered balloons, 49 feet tall by 39 feet wide, outfitted with transponders on the bottom. A high-speed Internet signal is beamed 60,000 feet to the nearest balloon, whereupon the signal is transmitted across the network of balloons and then down to users on the ground. They're absolutely beautiful: a dancing fleet of giant bubbles floating across the sky, bringing the Internet to underserved parts of the world to help them connect to family, information, and jobs. Test cases have been a huge success, including bringing connectivity to 10,000 in flood-ravaged Lima, Peru.

SOLVE FOR X

The team in the X division looks for the intersection of a big problem, a radical solution, and breakthrough technology. They start with a large problem in the world that, if solved, could improve the lives of millions or even billions of people. They imagine all kinds of crazy, insane, ludicrous solutions to that problem, then focus on one. This crazy, insane, ludicrous solution would remain an impossible fantasy without bringing it down to the ground, and this is where they look at breakthrough technology to see if they can build something to actually solve the problem in real terms.

Here's an example relating to home costs. In 2017, houses in Palo Alto had a median price of approximately $2.666 million. In a 2014 *Financial Times* article, Larry Page noted that, rather than exceeding $1 million, there's no reason why the median home in Palo Alto, in the heart of Silicon Valley, shouldn't cost $50,000. Of course, it's $2.6 million because of a tangled and complex set of issues including land availability, zoning laws, residents not wanting high-rise and high-density housing, tax laws, state laws, archaic rules around property ownership. So many elements come into play. So this is one of the next projects X is considering tackling. The solution to out-of-reach housing costs can be implemented around the world, not just in Palo Alto. It's a solvable problem. First address the restrictions, laws, and public objections. Then think high-density: Build 50 stories up. Or down. Then work on reducing costs even further with breakthrough building materials, construction methods, and technological innovations.

What about self-driving cars? On average, cars are parked 95 percent of the time. Just sitting there doing nothing, in parking lots or garages. But if one car were to be used by 20 people—driving itself to ferry those who need it when they need it, cars wouldn't sit idle. And there'd be a lot fewer cars. Think airplanes: You don't keep them on the ground. You keep them in the sky, flying passengers back and forth. The same model could be implemented for cars. The cost of car ownership would go down to $100 a month or so. Urban centers—without the need for the current number of parking lots, garages, and space dedicated to heavy traffic—could be completely revamped. Plus, those who aren't able to drive could get around, be independent. We just have to shift our thinking for the good of everyone and the good of our planet.

The point is, the sources of these issues may be complex, but the problems can be solved. What smart creatives do is to ask the question and then solve for x. That's where you take an equation that has a variable—x—and use the information around it to discover what x is. Like in algebra, to give a really simple example, you take $3x + 8 = 293$. Then you solve for x. Which is why the X division works.

How do you apply the idea of 10x innovation to your own life to increase your sense of the possible, the freedom that comes from going full-out? Think of yourself as a work in progress. Try a dream that seems so far out of reach it's ridiculous. Rewrite that story to allow for anything being possible. Then go for it. When you start taking action, find those with a similar mission. You don't have to go it alone. Don't worry about failing. Fail with pride. Failure leads to new possibilities. You don't need the most powerful technological tools to get your solution. But you do need to work with the powerful tools at your disposal—your mind, your body, your breath. And take your MEDS so you're receptive to joy, possibility, and expansion. Finally, while your solution may not affect billions of lives directly, if you're connected to your purpose, your joy, then those you come in contact with might feel a little bit better, and so might those *they* come in contact with, and so on.

WHAT ARE YOU CAPABLE OF BECOMING?

"Gopi," my father used to say to me when I was growing up, "it doesn't matter where you came *from* or what you came *with*. What matters is what you are capable of becoming."

Those words come back to me often, most especially in June 2002 when, after months of study, I became a United States citizen. Justice Ron White greeted those of us attending the naturalization ceremony with these words: "New citizens, please rise. Before you walked into this room, you were Irish, Italian, Indian, and many other nationalities. But as of this moment all of us are now Americans. Welcome to this great and diverse country of ours."

There I was, surrounded by people from 63 countries. On my left, a shy Vietnamese couple. Before me, a young Mexican family of six. On my right, a frail Irish grandmother. We looked different from each other. We spoke excitedly in Spanglish, Chinglish, and Hinglish. But we shared an experience that had begun long before that day with our answers to some unusual questions in a lengthy series of forms. Question 5: "Are you a spy?" Question 16: "Have you ever committed acts of moral turpitude?" (What is *that*?) My favorite, Question 44: "Do you intend to practice polygamy when you move to the United States?" But there was something else that brought us all together. One mission, one goal, one dream. The dream of freedom—the freedom to be our best selves and live our best lives. Isn't that what we all want?

As I sat there, listening to the words of Justice White, the words of my dad echoed in my heart. We'd been walking through our family's rice fields when he suddenly became emotional, put his hands on my shoulders, and said, "Gopi, you have traveled farther than anyone in our village ever has. You have gone beyond the limits of my imagination. All I could have given you was an education. But you have shown us what we are all capable of becoming. Your mother and I are very proud of you."

So I ask you, what are you capable of becoming? And what can you do to make it happen? You'll be astonished at what's possible.

BE
C😊MFORTABLE
WITH WHO
YOU ARE

Being comfortable enough in your own skin to take uncomfortable chances, to live your life in a way that's true to you, without apology, full-out, even if it means playing the fool, embarrassing yourself—that's when magic happens. The next step is sharing that magic, taking others along for the ride, each of you supporting and uplifting the other. When Buzz Aldrin took a leap so huge he watched Earth shrink in the rearview mirror before—more than 100 hours later—one probe skimmed the surface of the moon, he called out, "Contact light!"

When I first heard that he'd uttered those words, I thought he was talking about a beatific cosmic illumination sparked by contact with another world, not a blue light on the instrument panel.

To this day, when I take a leap into the unknown, I often hear those words—*contact light*—and picture that opening of dimensions, that galactic lightshow I first envisioned. Imagine that. Then imagine sharing that joyful moment with others, as Buzz Aldrin did when he shared his awe, his joy with 530 million viewers on planet Earth, lifting them up along with him.

IF Y😊U CAN
SPEAK, YOU
CAN SING

*The secret to happiness is freedom ... and
the secret to freedom is courage.*

— THUCYDIDES

When I was growing up, my dad said to me, "Gopi, when a door opens, always walk through it. Always." I didn't understand then that he was giving me a lesson for life, that his advice would help me reach my dreams.

One of my dreams was to speak in front of large groups, to capture their interest with my words, have them on the edge of their seats, laughing when I told a joke, moved by what I said. To persuade and influence. To make a difference. In grade school and high school I studied how my teachers moved and spoke in front of the class, what separated the engaging speakers from those who lost us at "Good morning, class." I was in awe of the ease and grace with which the good speakers moved and spoke. In my bedroom mirror after school, I replicated the facial expressions, body movements, elocution, and cadence of those who captivated us. In my late teens, I watched the grace with which the teachers at the ashram enthralled us, the way they strung words together, their animated expressions and well-timed pauses.

WEDNESDAY NIGHTS AT UNITY CHURCH

I didn't actually start studying public speaking until I moved to San Francisco from Hong Kong. I had no job, and I'd shelled out a good chunk of my $7,000 savings for a battered Honda and my first and last months' rent on a seedy apartment in an East Bay suburb populated largely by, as Pico Iyer wrote, "Afghan taxi drivers and half-fugitive South Asians." Immigrants starting their new lives, just as I was. I soon found a job building merchandising software for Safeway, a large supermarket chain.

Not long after I moved in, I saw a sign outside my neighborhood Unity Church advertising the next Toastmasters meeting, Wednesday at 6 P.M. I'd always wanted to join, and now the time just seemed right. I heard my father's voice in my head, *When a door opens, walk through it.* And that Wednesday, I walked to the church and into my first meeting, in one of Unity's Sunday school classrooms. Congoleum vinyl tile, chicken-wire glass windows, chairs set up in rows facing a desk and podium. The minute I walked into the room, just from the feel of the place, I was hooked. It took a couple of months before I felt ready to speak in front of the group. Until then, I sat in my plastic chair, facing the podium, watching speaker after speaker, studying every word, gesture, stressed syllable. They were so poised, so skilled. And they were all there to learn, practice, and improve by studying others and speaking themselves. I felt unbelievably happy, so excited by all I was learning.

My first speech was about taking a leap of faith. To prepare, I developed my content, then read it aloud, paring it down to the standard three minutes. I practiced for hours in front of my bathroom mirror. Once I had the content, I focused on my facial expressions, cadence, emphasis, pauses—all under the buzz of the canned light overhead. The night of my speech, I felt more excited than nervous. I walked to the podium, turned to the audience, took a deep breath, opened my mouth, and bombed. No one laughed at my jokes or smiled when I smiled; no one nodded when I struck a certain chord. I wasn't connecting. To be fair, you don't really bomb in Toastmasters. The clubs are extremely supportive and a great place to learn to speak—that's the idea, but they don't let you slide. They're not going to tell you you're excellent when you're not. They know you want to improve. And they're there to help. You get marked down on "ums" and "uhs," incorrect grammar, repeated words. The criticism's extremely constructive. You know exactly what to work on the next time. The good news was, I had plenty of opportunity for improvement. And I loved being up there, speaking, even if I felt the energy in the room flatten with each word I spoke. And I got better. I was determined to get better.

After weeks, months, of practice at Toastmasters, I started to give speeches to larger groups for work. At first, they didn't go all that well either. People politely applauded and handed out faint praise—"Thank you" or "Nice speech"—but I knew deep down that my words had barely made a dent. I can tell from the energy in the room how a speech of mine is going. Plus, I also have tangible proof: my selfie rating system. After a speech, if people have connected with what I've said, they often come up and ask to take a selfie with me to post on social media. The number of selfies taken for each minute of my speech tells me how good the speech was. If it's not so great, there might be one to two selfies per stage minute. If it's really good and moves people, I might score 3.79 per minute, or nearly 40 for a 10-minute speech. Back then, I was scoring zero.

It didn't matter. I continued to go to Toastmasters. I still do. I've been a member for 20 years and continue to practice and learn more skills and work with my coaches. It's a passion and a process—for me, a multi-decade process, during which, in addition to Toastmasters, I've taken advantage of every bit of training I can get. I watch speeches on YouTube, pay attention to good speakers at conferences, study podcasts, pore over articles on good speaking that I find on the Internet. Speaking is a skill that anyone can acquire if they're willing to put in the time. For each major speech I give, I put in two hours for each minute I'll be on stage speaking. For the Toastmasters International World Championship of Public Speaking, I put in 30 hours per minute. I've made Toastmasters meetings, trainings, and my own speaking engagements a life priority. It's not always easy, especially with travel and overbooked days. Still, I've managed to put in the time, often watching and listening to others on my phone, and I've been richly rewarded.

If you have a dream, even if you have all the natural talent in the world, you have to develop that talent. Learn the skills. Surround yourself with those who share your interest, work with a coach or mentor. Carve out the time. And practice, practice, practice. If you love what you're doing, if it holds meaning for you, resonates with who you are, it will be not a grind, but a joy.

THE WORLD CHAMPIONSHIP
OF PUBLIC SPEAKING

Ten days after I returned from India, after my father passed away, I flew to Vancouver to compete in the World Championship of Public Speaking. The competition had started in February with more than 30,000 contestants from 142 countries, and after the quarterfinals it was down to 100 semifinalists who would go head-to-head in 10 semifinal tracks in Vancouver. My track had a man from St. Kitts, a Jamaican woman representing Canada, another woman from the Caribbean representing the United Kingdom, an American man representing Korea, a Korean man representing the Philippines, a woman from Zimbabwe representing Australia, and an Indian American, me, as one of the U.S. representatives. Clearly, competitive public speakers are adventurous spirits who are willing to stray far from their home countries.

Wearing the shirt my father had said he liked when I visited him in the ICU the day he passed, I gave one of my best speeches ever, hitting every note I wanted to (and that my coaches had asked me to). Five days before the competition, my head coach suggested that I change one of my two speeches, making it a tribute to my dad. I did. The day before the competition, a past world champion, having heard me practice, advised me to go into the semis with that speech. So I did. It was very emotional for me. As I spoke, I could feel my dad there with me. During the acknowledgements section, when they asked me whom I wanted to thank, I said, "I thank my coaches, and I thank my dad," and then I couldn't continue. It was a moving and profound moment for me and my family, some of whom were watching live from India. The audience went quiet. In hushed silence, they watched a deeply personal moment unfold on stage. I cried. They applauded.

I didn't make it to one of the 10 coveted spots in the finals. The person who won from my semifinal round, Kevin Stamper, went on to win third place in the championship. He's a young career pastor from Florida who's been giving inspirational speeches every week of his adult life. As I jokingly told my friends, "It's like being drawn into the same round as Usain Bolt, and he also had God on his side. You can't compete with that!"

The person who became the World Champion of Public Speaking 2017 was also a career professional speaker, an Indian from Singapore named Manoj Vasudevan. In a remarkable coincidence, he's from the same town— Thiruvananthapuram, Kerala—I lived in growing up. He's from my high school and the same engineering school as my brother. There were six Indians in the semis and three in the finals. Thanks to the British legacy, India is emerging as an unlikely superpower in competitive public speaking in English. It is like watching the 100-meter finals in a world open track event and noticing that half the field is from Jamaica, or seeing all the Kenyans in the front of the pack at the New York City Marathon. While India wins very few medals in the Olympics, it produces world champions in some improbable competitive arenas like public speaking, spelling bees, snooker, chess, and badminton.

Overall, I'm thrilled with my six-month journey this year and the 17 years of competing from the time I started and couldn't make it past the first round. It has made me a better speaker, for sure, and I know my father was glowing with pride. Within days after competing, I started my preparations for 2018. I'll keep going.

SINGING IN THE CLOSET

Speaking wasn't my only dream. Since I was 10, I'd dreamed of becoming a singer. Whenever I heard my favorite song, I'd belt it out, pick up my air guitar, and shred the chords. But I never followed up on my dream as I got older. I'm sure all of you have had a childhood dream that you didn't follow up on. Maybe it was the voices in your head that stopped you. You know the ones: *You don't have any talent. You don't know where to start. You're not good enough.* I heard the same voices in my head. With good reason, I told myself. My family had no singing talent. *Maybe farther back,* I thought. So I peered *waaay* back into my family tree—my mom's side, dad's side. Zero. Zippo. Nada. No singers. So now I had the weight of my family legacy stamped into my gene pool and on my forehead. The voice in my head echoed: *The Kallayil family is cursed with no singers.*

Then, 10 years ago, I walked into a Starbucks in San Francisco. On the way out, chai in hand, I saw a stack of advertisements. The word *sing* jumped out at me, so I picked one up. "If you can speak, you can sing," it read. It sounded a bit ridiculous, so I crumpled it up, tossed it into the trash, and walked away. Two steps from the door, I stopped in my tracks. *I just trashed my dream.* I rushed back and dug through the bin (which surprisingly didn't faze me). I pulled out the wadded piece of paper, smoothed it out on the counter, then called the number.

"Hello, this is Julia. I teach beginners. After six lessons, you'll be singing in public." I hesitated. Then I thought of my dad's words again—"When a door opens, Gopi, *always* walk through it"—and I signed up. And as she promised, after six lessons I gave my first public performance. I sang

"Amazing Grace." If you'd been there, you would have seen that my audience was huge. Four classmates, four loved ones dragged there, two dogs that howled when I sang. Despite the dogs, singing in front of a group felt amazing. So incredibly freeing.

Next, I tackled one of the items on my list of 100 things I wanted to do with my life that I wrote about earlier: sing with a band onstage. I found my opportunity at Burning Man a year or so after launching my singing career in front of my audience of 10. Performing at Burning Man: no audition required, just enthusiasm. Show up with your instrument and play, however bad you are. The same holds for singing. I sang with a really talented Germany-and-U.K.-based band I knew that played *kirtan*, a genre I'm very drawn to. I walked up on stage as though I did it every day. I wasn't nervous, just excited. I couldn't stop grinning. Burning Man was an incredibly safe place for my first time onstage. Because of their radical inclusivity, there are no spectators. Everyone is a participant. Everyone is a performer. All of Burning Man is one giant stage for anyone to perform whatever they want to do at any time. Even if you're devoid of talent, which, of course, I thought I was.

Getting up on that stage wasn't like speaking in front of a large audience with my selfie-meter clocking in at zero. At Burning Man, you're deluded into thinking you have a fine, attentive audience, but if you lean in closer, you'll realize they've just been wandering in the desert, dehydrated, then stumbled into this place to get a little bit of shade, saying to each other, "Yeah, man, this is kind of cool. Let's check it out." Then, dazed (which can look a lot like blissed out from the stage), they head for a beanbag couch and flop.

Between Julia and my friends at Burning Man, I was falling seriously in love with singing—onstage, offstage. I didn't care. For five years, I sang anywhere and everywhere I could—everything from folk to blues to Indian music, especially *kirtan*, which I often performed with my good friend, Ananta, who is a music producer. One day, Ananta called with this crazy idea. "Gopi," he said, "if we collaborate on performing and producing and bring in other kirtan musicians, we could do an album."

I couldn't believe my ears. "Really?" Another dream.

"Sure. If we work on it, we can."

I heard my father's words.

The door had opened slightly, and I stepped through and let the magic unfold. I converted my walk-in closet into a recording studio. After two years of recording, rerecording, re-rerecording, our group, Kirtan Lounge, released its first album, *Nectar of Devotion*. Then a second, *Precious Jewels*. We've sold a whopping 300 copies of our first and not quite that many yet of our second. A far bit from platinum. But then, out of the blue, as you read in an earlier chapter, Jewel's team offered to sponsor us for a Grammy in five categories. That, in and of itself, was huge, that our humble album was considered worthy enough for a member of the Recording Academy to say, "Let's enter it for the Grammys." Wow. If we could get this far with an album recorded among the shirts and jeans in my closet, imagine what's possible!

How many of you have a dream you've thrown into the trash can? Is there a story in your head that's stopping you? Dig your dreams out of the trash. Take that first small step. In life, you'll experience a number of doors. Some are open. Some are closed. Just remember, when a door opens, *always* walk through it. Let the magic unfold.

G☺ WANDER

When you are inspired by some great purpose, some extraordinary project, all your thoughts break their bonds. Your mind transcends limitations, your consciousness expands in every direction, and you find yourself in a new, great, and wonderful world. Dormant forces, faculties and talents become alive, and you discover yourself to be a greater person by far than you ever dreamed yourself to be.

— YOGA SUTRAS OF PATANJALI

Curiosity and exploration are part of being a happy human and certainly a part of my own happiness. They completely open your world. Don't worry that you haven't mastered the language, don't know all the routes, are ordering from a menu you can't read—that's part of the experience. Think of a toddler wandering around. Everything's new. They're constantly exploring, wobbling off, throwing toys. When you wander around new places, feed your curiosity, in a sense, you're like a toddler; the difference is, when you're completely comfortable in your skin, when you live your life from that place of trust, unlike a toddler whose home base is Mom and Dad, your home base is even closer: at your core.

I'll often set off for someplace new just for the experience, which is what I did after the three days of meetings following my weekend hotel retreat in Tokyo. I took the suggestion of my colleague Wakana and my friend Pico Iyer and headed for Kōya-san, one of the most sacred sites in the country, to get a taste of ancient, deep, mysterious Japan. The place is practically inaccessible, but it sounded interesting, and I'd never been there, so off I went.

It wasn't an easy trip. First, a high-speed Nozomi bullet train whisked me from Tokyo Station to Shin-Osaka Station, where the Midosuji Line subway hauled me to Namba Station. The local train, the Nankai Electric Railway, then shuttled me to Gokurakubashi Station, at which point a cable car dragged me up the mountain and back down. Then a bus ferried me from the Gokurakubashi Station to the Karukayado-mae bus stop, in the town center.

At 5 P.M., six hours after leaving Tokyo, I stood alone in the middle of the town, which had shut down for the night—not a soul on the street, no taxis anywhere. There are 117 temples in Kōya-san, and 53 of them take in guests. I wandered up the cobblestone street until I found the Myoo-in, the temple where I'd made a reservation. I checked in, then followed one of the monks to my room. He handed me what looked like a user's manual of ancient customs. I bowed, stored my suitcase, then went downstairs in search of directions to the Okunoin Cemetery, which Pico had insisted I must see at twilight. I searched for someone to help me, but I didn't understand a word of what anyone was saying, grasp a thing about what was going on or what I was supposed to do.

I breathed, went with it, and finally, thank goodness, a kind man who spoke a bit of English came out of the kitchen and offered to help. His dress was different from that of the monks I'd seen so far. "Are you one of the monks?" I asked him. "No, no, no," he said. "I am ordinary person." I nodded, wondering, *Where do I stack in that hierarchy of ordinary person, extraordinary person, monk? What are the categorizations below ordinary person that I am relegated to forever, cursed to live in?*

I asked him how to get to the cemetery. He told me there were no taxis available at that time of day, so I tried to figure out the bus system, which was nearly impossible because, as I mentioned, I don't speak or read the language.

I went out into the streets and found a shop selling herbal medicines that was still open. With the assistance of Google Translate, I tried asking the kind, polite, and gracious shopkeeper for help. I kept pointing to where I thought the cemetery was. She kept pointing in another direction, saying, "Go there, go there. Go to *daido. Daido.*" At the time, I didn't know what exactly she was saying. I later realized she was telling me to go to the central temple because it's well lit in the dark and one can enjoy it, as opposed to walking into the dark graveyard.

I ended up not going that night. I learned I could find my way on foot, but realized if I got lost in the graveyard, I probably couldn't find my way out, and I'd have to spend the night amidst 200,000 graves in the freezing Japanese winter on top of a mountain, That wouldn't make me at all happy. I know what makes me happy. At that moment, it was the thought of a nice, warm futon bed, donning a *yukata* for the walk to the baths, then sitting naked in one of the hot tubs.

I went back to my room, where there was no futon. Just a narrow tatami mat, a *goza*, to serve as my bed. There was nothing to do, no one to talk to. Dinner was an hour away—a set time for everyone. While I waited, I picked up the user's manual, lay down on the goza, and pored over the guidelines. The manual was written in Japanese with English translations, and cartoonlike illustrations

throughout. I read the instructions—every piece of eti-
quette you could imagine for the entire temple. All the
things you should do in the morning. What they served
for breakfast. How you eat it. What you do at the temple.
When you should show up. All uniquely nuanced, including two pages about how to wrap yourself in a yukata,
which you wore to the *osen*, the natural spring baths,
and to bed.

A yukata is basically a bathrobe. In the United States,
if they put a bathrobe in the room, you just take it off
the hanger, put it on, and tie the belt. Done. Finis. Not in
Japan. You must cross the left side over the right in front
(right over left is for corpses), make sure the hemline on
the right and left sides are even and the gap at the neck-
line isn't too revealing. Men tie the sash one way, women
another. "Never wear the yukata to the morning temple
ceremony," I read. That was a strict no-no, like showing
up at a job interview in red silk pajamas. Everything was
so very precisely defined. Every piece of the manual was
highly useful because it's a different cultural experience,
and I had no idea what was correct, offensive, or completely forbidden. The manual was absolutely fascinating.

The next morning, I was walking down to the temple
for my meditation when these four guys, about 20 years
old, came walking down the path wearing their yukatas,
probably thinking, in all their cultural innocence, that
they were dressed most appropriately. As they approached,
I could hear one saying to the others, "Dude, we look like
Crouching Tiger, Hidden Dragon, you know?" For them,
being in the monastery in the mountains of Japan was like
being in the hit *wuxia* movie, a genre of pseudo-historical
martial arts—set in China. Not Japan. They were going to
the temple, wearing their yukatas, which is like wearing

lingerie to church in the United States. I stopped them and told them they had to change.

We talked for a few minutes. They'd all gone to the University of Colorado a few years earlier and were meeting for a reunion. Two Americans, one German, and one guy from South America. I was baffled by their choice of location for a reunion. A remote, forbidding mountain hamlet in Japan with 117 temples and a high-traffic graveyard isn't exactly Las Vegas or Ibiza.

They went back to their rooms, and I went on to the temple, fantasizing about what the monks would have thought if those guys had worn their yukatas to the temple. Would they have said something? Kicked them out? Or, this being Japan, where everyone is so very polite, would they have suffered in silence because it would have been even more upsetting to throw out the visitors? Would the monks then have had to meditate for the next three days just to find peace in this terrible situation because in the 567-year history of this temple, this faux pas had never been committed?

I guess I'll never know. The point is, while you wander, comfortable with who you are, you have to be mindful of *where* you are, respectful of the situation and customs, so as not to make others uncomfortable. That way, you open yourself up to connecting with those around you.

OKUNOIN CEMETERY

That evening, rested from my trip, I swallowed my worry about getting lost among the graves and set out on foot for the graveyard, a tribute to Kūkai, the famous Buddhist monk and founder of the Shingon (True Word) school of Buddhism. In 816, wanting to build a base from which to spread his teachings, legend has it he threw a pitchfork from China that landed in what is now Kōya-san. Traveling on the train the day before, I'd wanted to curse him a little bit for throwing the fork in the direction he had, because in 2016, it was so hard to get to. *If it is this hard now, how did he even find the place his pitchfork allegedly landed 1,200 years ago? How did he make his way up the mountain? There were no electric trains, no cable cars. He must have walked. How many days did it take him?* And on and on, my thoughts spinning, I entertained myself all the way up the mountain.

And now I was stumbling along the road, long past twilight, in the eerie ancient cedar forest, trying to find the cemetery, cursing Pico a little bit for insisting I come here, arcing my phone in the air like a wand as I tried to snag a signal, attempting to plot my route on Street View, memorizing the route, turning my phone to flashlight mode to shine a path ahead of me. And finally, finally, I was at the Ichi-no-Hashi bridge, where you cross from one world to another. I entered cautiously, a little spooked, I admit, and then I stopped, mesmerized by the ancient cedars standing among the eroded tombstones, moss-covered torii gates, memorials, the thousands of Jizo statues. The history. It felt a bit creepy, but more than that, it felt sacred. If it were summer, I might have stayed the night. I was that taken with the beauty and the story behind it.

Before Kūkai died, he told his disciples to bury him in the little valley that is now the cemetery so he could have some peace and quiet. That lasted about 32 days, at most, because, wanting to be near such a famous monk, every Japanese emperor, admiral of the navy, and lowly official of a prefecture far away in some peaceful rice-growing village expressed a dying request to be buried next to him. For centuries. Now there's a teeming graveyard of 200,000. This guy has no peace. He's surrounded by madness. And because of that madness, tourists, travelers, everyone comes to visit. The graveyard is overrun by people aboveground and below, visible and not so visible. One of the most spectacular mausoleums was erected by a Japanese termite company to pay honor to and ask for forgiveness for all the termites and pests that their products had exterminated.

There's the irony to this story. Kūkai located the most remote place he could possibly find, one that's incredibly hard to get to, and before he died, said, "Just bury me in this valley and I'll have some peace." It didn't work out that way. And I have no idea how they brought all those caskets up the mountain.

NO BREAKFAST

When I got back down the mountain, I stayed at a closet hotel I'd found on the web. My door opened into the room, inches from the tiny one-person bed with a foot of space on either side. There was a little bathroom, a communal hot-tub bath. And you just slept there, got up in the morning, and left. The next morning, I went down for breakfast. There was food sitting out, ready to be picked up, buffet style, but the receptionist, who spoke some English, said, "No, no, no. No more breakfast. Past ten o'clock."

If I'd preordered a breakfast the night before, I would have been fine, but I hadn't done that. I hadn't known I was supposed to. And I was hungry. "I'll pay for it," I said, opening my wallet. "Please, let me buy breakfast."

The receptionist shook her head. "No, no, no. The food is for the people who bought breakfast last night."

"But it's ten o'clock. You've already shut down for the morning, so clearly those people aren't coming."

Anywhere else, if there's food sitting there, you pay your money and you take the food. But she wouldn't let me touch it. I was starving. I wanted to eat, but I couldn't.

"You're going to throw that out," I argued.

She nodded. "Yes."

"Okay, then let me pay for it and eat it."

"No, no, no, no. This already paid for, other people come."

"But it's ten o'clock. They're not going to come."

We went around and around with our circular logic. I wasn't getting anywhere. I did not get any food.

It's all very procedural in Japan, very orderly. You go by the rules. You cannot deviate. But I didn't know the rules.

I suppose that whole experience of not knowing what people are saying to you, not understanding what they want you to do, coming up against no and no and no and not being able to make yourself understood is what toddlers go through every day. They get up, stumble and bump their way across their world, put things in their mouths, chew on them, spit them out. Explore. That's how they learn. It's no picnic. They're constantly on sensory overload.

Towering creature in their faces—cooing, eyes lit up, singing ridiculous songs. The toddler must be thinking, *Dude, none of this is necessary. Why are you doing whatever you're doing? Just leave me alone (but don't go too far, because, you know, I'm two).* To feel free to explore our world, we need a sense of home base too, a safe place. First and foremost within ourselves, but also in our workplace and with friends and loved ones.

I felt that kind of learning and discovering and not quite knowing what to expect on this trip. There was an element of frustration and confusion, but also a sense of joy in a whole new world before me. I feel that sense of joy, of discovery, at work every day, where we're encouraged to be curious. To be happy, inquisitive, just delighted by the unexpected and sometimes even by the difficulty that comes with all this wandering, bumping, creative flow. In the process of exploring uncharted waters, we all find ourselves in uncomfortable circumstances, situations, and outcomes that aren't what we expected. But you can't let that stop you. Let your curiosity lead you. Expose yourself to whatever shows up. Sometimes it can be a little painful, but that's okay. Pick it up, chew on it, and if you don't like it, try something else.

SURR☺UND
YOURSELF
WITH
HAPPINESS

Just as a diamond can only be polished
by another diamond, it is only through genuine,
all-out engagement with others that people
can polish their character, and help each
other to reach greater heights.

— DAISAKU IKE, BUDDHIST PHILOSOPHER,
PEACEBUILDER, EDUCATOR, AUTHOR, POET

One of the most important keys to maintaining and nurturing happiness is to surround yourself with others who are happy, to let that happiness in, take part in the joy, let it fuel your creativity and sense of possibility. I had an exceptional experience with what this energy can foster in 2017 when I attended the weeklong European Youth Summit for Young Leaders in the European Union. It was held at the M.A. Center, one of Amma Mata Amritanandamayi Devi's ashrams. Known as the hugging saint, she's one of the most respected humanitarians and spiritual leaders in the world. Three hundred young people, ages

15 to 30, representing 24 nationalities, attended, all of us nestled in a mountain valley at the height of summer, the week filled with beautiful, long days when the sun doesn't set until around 9:30 P.M.

The summit is dedicated to empowering young people to contribute to a peaceful and sustainable world and become compassionate leaders with a sense of tolerance, solidarity, and global responsibility. It's a collaboration between the European Union and Embracing the World, founded by Amma. The name of the partnership is AYUDH, or Amrita Yuva Dharma Dhara, a Sanskrit phrase that means "the youth that perpetuates the wheel of dharma (righteousness)"; it's also known as Youth for Unity, Diversity, and Humanity. The organization believes that personal transformation lies at the heart of real change in the world. In addition to cultural, social, political, and ecological perspectives, it incorporates a spiritual dimension when addressing each daily topic of the summit.

It's a polyglot environment—300 people from 25 countries, speaking many different languages, communicating through translators and often the participants themselves who translate for each other. There is just a great energy, wholesomeness, beauty, playfulness that is quite evident when you throw all these people together. The summit opens their hearts. That's the main purpose.

UNITED FOR A COMMON CAUSE

Each year there's a theme. In 2017, it was "Educate. Cultivate. Participate." Participants explored the theme through hands-on experience and interactive learning in three categories—peaceful and nonviolent societies, sustainable lifestyles, and European and global citizenship—with a focus on collaboratively developing follow-up projects that can be implemented in local communities. International speakers and panelists addressed participants and facilitated the more than 20 workshops, and I was lucky enough to be one of them.

This was the second year that I'd gone. Both years I'd paid my way and taken time off work to be able to contribute, volunteer, teach, and engage with the energy of this incredible program. I love interacting with the participants. This is where I want to be. This is meaningful. It just makes me happy.

At the 2017 summit, I spoke to the entire group about imagining radical solutions to problems they encounter, and how innovation can come from anywhere and everywhere. I then facilitated a series of short workshops focused on these ideas. Before I started speaking, I looked around the room, taking in the open faces, the intense focus. I'd seen and talked to many of the participants outside the workshops and been amazed by the fast friendships they'd formed, often despite language barriers. I felt absolutely certain that these people would initiate great change for humanity, and I felt honored to be a part of this group.

I wanted to start off by inspiring them. "You're starting on these projects," I said. "You think you have just a small idea in your head, and you might think it's never going to be big, never have any significant impact." I could see I was hitting home, but my point was to encourage, so I said, "Everyone is equally capable of amazing ideas." Then I laid the groundwork to speak about Google's Nine Principles of Innovation. "How many of you use Google?" I asked. "Just one product. Raise your hand." Every single person there raised one hand. "How many of you use two products—maybe YouTube and Google? Raise two hands."

Everybody raised both hands. "Everybody who uses three products, such as Google Maps, YouTube, and Google, stand up." Everybody stood—both hands held up. "If you use four products, start waving." Everybody waved. "If you use five products, start jumping." Now the whole room was jumping up and down.

When they sat down again, I said, "You come from so many countries, and yet, clearly, these products have such a big impact on your lives. But this whole thing began in two guys' heads. And those two guys started this company when they were in their early to mid-twenties. That's the median age of all of you in this room." I told them Google started as an idea, just as their projects were. "At the end of this summit, you'll each receive one thousand euros to seed-fund your projects in the community. You might think that's not enough money to do anything. But let me tell you, Google was started on zero dollars. These were Ph.D. students at Stanford. They had very little money. They scraped together what they could, rented a nearby garage from their friend Susan Wojcicki, and spent months day and night, building a website on Stanford's server. That little white box where you could go and search only in English. The first version of Google: zero dollars. Nowhere near the thousand euros you'll receive."

I showed them a picture of the outside of the garage where the company was founded. Then the inside. "The smallest of ideas can lead to some of the most world-changing innovations," I told them, "so don't discount them." I talked to them about how we approach big problems at Google and the Nine Principles of Innovation, focusing on "Aim for 10x" and "Fail well." I discussed some of Google's bigger projects—self-driving cars, bringing the Internet to everyone, reducing waste in the world. "They're working on solving big problems that will affect billions. And you're working on projects that address some of the most urgent issues facing our world today—integration, religious tolerance, cultural understanding, civic engagement, sustainable lifestyles. At the end of the day," I said, "all projects take on a deeper meaning when you have a sense of *what* you're solving for, the *why*. People do it because they want to make a difference in this world." I told them that's exactly why they were here in this room right now. That's exactly what they were doing with their projects.

In our high-speed world of information overload, the demands placed on young people, the competing bids for their attention, make them especially susceptible to being dragged off in different directions. One teenager from Europe might be brought into a place like the youth summit and asked to think about sustainability and nonviolence, while someone else with a young, impressionable mind may be drawn to something on the other end of the spectrum, feeling compelled to travel to Syria to become a terrorist. The people at the conference were given something meaningful and wholesome to think about and focus on, and this centered them, fostered the strong sense of purpose that had led them to the summit.

One team was working on reducing waste in the world by giving consumers a choice about what they buy. It's socially conscious consumerism. There's a famous video, *The Story of Stuff*, that points out that when you buy a shirt or a shoe or a book, there's a backstory. You may not realize how much work went into making that product, the materials, the cost, the child labor used. If you become aware of the backstory, sometimes you might not want to buy that product. You say, "No. I don't want any part of it."

Think of the diamond necklaces and earrings worn at a ball in New York City that look so beautiful catching and throwing the light. If you trace those diamonds back to their source, you may learn they were used by armed groups to finance conflict and commit grave human rights abuses. When you learn the story, the beauty is diminished if not annihilated. Those shiny diamonds may be tainted by blood.

So, this team working on socially conscious consumerism came up with an idea for an app similar to My Fitness Pal. You'd hold your phone up to an item that you're considering buying, and it tells you the story behind it. This is an amazing idea. Imagine the change it could effect. They haven't built it yet, but that's the idea they came up with. This is what I mean when I say it's just incredible to witness their energy, youthfulness, creativity, willingness to risk. You should have seen them. The joy, the sense of peace and hope in the possibility that this app could make a difference, and what that difference might look like in the world, the love and concern for the planet and humanity—that's what I mean by opening hearts.

AN INTENTION FOR PEACE

The first year I went to the summit, I was a little apprehensive given the age group. I felt sure the attendees would see me as this older adult and wouldn't pay attention, but no, they were so loving and very much leaning into the experience and just lovely to talk to.

Because the M.A. Center is an ashram, during the summit there are yoga classes twice a day and chanting in the evenings in an Indian musical genre called *Bhajans*, which are participative call and response. It's radically inclusive and everyone is encouraged to join in. And because of the spiritual element of the organization, there's a natural self-selection going on with the type of people who attend. About half these participants come from fairly devotional families, meaning their parents are Amma devotees, so they go for the meditation and the chanting. Their parents may practice yoga. Many of them practice yoga too, so they have that grounding already. On top of that, they are involved, curious, open, and leaning. Not every single one. Some don't engage in the programs and just hang around. It's bound to happen, but for the most part, they're highly committed and engaged.

Besides the yoga classes and chanting, the workshops in public speaking, leadership, and problem solving, there are sessions focusing on different types of art and music, which end up fueling the creative process. It's an amazingly joyful environment—it's peaceful, it's a farm, and it's got these incredible young people running around, bringing optimism and bubbling energy. Teaching them, being with them, participating in their activities, just boosted my own energy and level of happiness around it. Most of the joy, though, that everyone felt, came from a sense of hope for humanity. Great things are possible.

One of my favorite parts of the day was the evening ceremony, at sunset, when we would all gather by the lake to meditate. A few of the participants would play instruments and sing. A German boy, Nath Hirsch, played the harmonium. Andrea, a mellifluous singer from the Basque region of Spain, sang beautifully. A voice actor of Indian origin from the United Kingdom played the percussive *tabla*. Shubamirta, a swami from India, the director of European operations for Embracing the World, would lead all of us in chanting, *"Lokah samastah sukhino bhavantu"*— *May all beings in this world be happy*—over and over again.

We'd continue to chant while each participant lit a floating candle, walked down to the lake, knelt at the shore, and set his or her candle in the water while sending their intention for peace to somewhere else in the world. By that time, it would be growing dark and you'd be able to see these candles floating out on the lake. It was a lovely ceremony. Everyone would be completely taken by it, some people shedding gentle tears, some sobbing. Something about the ceremony must have touched them. The incredible joy, calmness, peace, possibility that was emerging was so beautiful to behold.

Happiness may not be very complicated. In this instance, the pure environment, the community, the incredible opportunity, fostered the sense of joy. But this is a choice we make. We all have skills. We have time. We have the resources on some level to put ourselves in situations where we're doing something in a meaningful way, having an impact on our own lives and the lives of others. We make those choices from what's available to us. The world is a big place. Find something that interests you, that you love doing, and give it a chance to develop. When you surround yourself with positive energy and people who have a similar intention and focus, anything is possible.

REACH OUT
AND TOUCH

Every time you smile at someone, it is an action of love, a gift to that person, a beautiful thing.

— MOTHER TERESA

In our hyper-connected, yet often disconnected world, we can take advantage of technology to connect with others and bring us closer. Through social media, we might acknowledge a friend or send a warm comment. Maybe we come across a piece of music on YouTube that we know a friend will love, and we text or e-mail it to that friend, which I often do. Or we send a quick text message to reach out in a way that's thoughtful and nonintrusive, one that doesn't necessarily require a response.

During the Paris terrorist attacks in 2015, I was able to stay present with my dear friend Amandine, who was on a U.N. project in Haiti, assisting with elections. She's originally from Bordeaux, with many friends in Paris, and was very distressed. I couldn't be with her, which was hard, but I was able to send short text messages to let her know I was there for her. I was even able to jump on Skype and speak to her for five minutes, and thank God for technology, because I was able to see her, to look her in the eye, and get an even stronger sense of how she was feeling.

It's these tiny gestures, these acts of service—saying *I'm here, I'm noticing, I'm checking in, I'm thinking of you*— and of being present across time zones and borders that allow us to use technology to our advantage to touch someone, connect, draw closer. Without it, we couldn't communicate with each other to the extent and frequency that we now can.

But then there comes a point when we need to be physically close, to be in the presence of another to feel alive, vibrant, and connected. As Thich Nhat Hanh, whom I was lucky enough to host for a talk at Google, said, "If you love someone, the greatest gift you can give them is your presence."

With all the advances in outer technology, our inner technology holds fast. One thing has been true for the 200,000 plus years we have been in our current form. (Actually, as I write this, we've been around for 267,443 years, 3 months, and 14 days, to be precise. Google told me this.) Human beings still need to be *in each other's presence.* To feel that presence, we need to hear a voice directly, not over a telephone or an electronic device. We need to be able to look into the other person's eyes, not through a camera or computer screen, but with nothing more than air between. And, often, we need our bodies to touch, to feel each other's skin. The fundamental indication of this truth is the relationship between little babies and their parents. While traveling parents can connect with their very young children at home via video conferencing, nothing takes the place of feeling the actual warmth from their child's body, or, for children, seeing their father's eyes crinkling when he smiles, or hearing the sound of their mother's voice—laughter, a silly song, soothing words.

THE HEALING POWER OF HUGS

In *The Upward Spiral: Using Neuroscience to Reverse the Course of Depression, One Small Change at a Time,* Alex Korb discusses the calming effect of hugs. "A hug," he writes, "especially a long one, releases a neurotransmitter and hormone oxytocin, which reduces the reactivity of the amygdala." In other words, oxytocin informs the amygdala (our brain's center for fear, anxiety, and aggression) to stand down. So we feel safe, calm, happy.

The United States is fairly open with affection. We often greet friends and family with a hug. In my family, and in the Indian culture, there's a lot less of that type of contact. But when my dad passed, the comfort of touch and proximity was a support for us all. Before the cremation, everyone—friends, family, neighbors—was breaking down, sobbing. But as the eldest son, and supposedly the most grounded person, I was expected to maintain my composure while going through my own grief. I was standing in the crowd, dry-eyed, doing my best to keep it together, when my sister walked up to me, crying, and hugged me. It wasn't words that comforted me that day, but the strength and support provided by touch.

The morning after the cremation, we were all pretty exhausted. I was also jet-lagged and woke up later than the others. When I finally went downstairs, I found the entire family in my parents' bedroom, gathered around my mother, who was sitting up in the same bed she'd slept in for so many years with my dad. When I walked into the room, she smiled, patted the bed right next to her, and said, "Come, sit here." It was clear to me that she needed the strength provided by proximity. A sense of *I want all my kids around me. And I want you, as my eldest son, to sit right next to me because now I feel safe. I feel taken care of. I feel comfortable, I'm not alone.*

Before leaving for the U.S., I went to see a very good friend from my undergrad days. We talked, and I gave him an update on everything that was going on. As I walked to the door to leave, the past few days caught up with me. I suddenly felt overwhelmed with emotion. As I crossed the threshold, tears running down my cheeks, my friend called me to come back into the living room with the exclusive purpose of giving me one big last hug before I left. That one small gesture calmed me, and I was able to walk out the door a little lighter than I'd been moments before.

These gestures may seem small, but they grounded me, and let love and connection in, during a time when I was so keenly feeling the loss of my father. And with my mother and sister, my family, the comfort we felt by being close, gathered in the same room, I can't put into words.

ARE YOU SMILING AT *ME*?

Smiling doesn't just make us feel better. British researchers found that one smile can stimulate the brain as much as eating up to 2,000 chocolate bars or receiving up to 16,000 pounds sterling. Plus, research has shown that thanks to the working of mirror neurons—brain cells that respond equally when we perform an action or witness someone else perform that action—we often respond to the act of smiling by imitating it and smiling ourselves. Joy gone viral!

During my first month at Google, I was asked to attend a meeting that had to do with the business area I was working in. Senior leadership needed to make a decision, and they wanted to give our team an update and get our input. For these types of meetings, they take small groups at a time, and it's a quick-fire exchange for 5 to 10 minutes. During these meetings, the senior execs maintain that stern corporate leadership presence. As we filed into the room and settled into our seats, the senior execs were all preoccupied with the meeting agenda and didn't make eye contact.

But Omid Kordestani, at that time the Senior Vice President of Global Sales, looked around, and when he saw me, I'm sure I had "new guy" written all over me—that most vulnerable, unsure, insecure, least-important-person-in-the-room vibe. And also that sense of insecurity that has stayed with me for my entire Google career, and for good reason: I am the least smart person in this room. He must have sensed it, because he gave a broad, warm smile—not a quick, polite corporate smile, but a smile of one human being genuinely acknowledging another. I could feel the kindness. I felt seen and welcomed. A smile that took no more than two seconds. Tops. And that memory has stayed with me for years, bringing up the same feelings each time I remember it. Such resonance from one small gesture, one human to another.

When I'd been at Google a while, I was sitting in the cafeteria of our San Francisco office. Margo Georgiadis, who was then the president of Google Americas and therefore my superboss, walked briskly through the cafeteria, an entourage racing to keep up. She was on her way to present at an all-hands meeting in the large room directly across from the cafeteria. As she walked, she glanced in my direction and flashed a big beaming smile. Margo and I had had a few interactions here and there, and I figured she might know who I was, but when I saw her smile, I thought, *She's smiling at somebody behind me,* and turned to see who it was. No one was there. I turned back, and there she was, still smiling. At me. And not only was she smiling at me, she was making a beeline straight for me.

My heart sank. *Oh, my God, she must think I'm Shankar, that brilliant engineer from the Indian Institute of Technology who's working on the search ad quality algorithm and she has a question she wants to discuss with him and I'll be like a blithering idiot because in three seconds she'll know I know nothing about the topic and I'm not that person.* Still, when she came to stand in front of me, I stood up. "Hey, Gopi," she said. "Great to see you. I've been hearing great things about you from the team. I've heard you've been doing amazing things in all the executive summits." Something like that. And I thought, *She knows it's me, Gopi, not Shankar.* And I got that feeling of being seen (plus a smile and a hug).

CONNECTING

Sometimes there's no hug, no smile, but there's still that strong feeling of connection that you can only get from being in the same room with others. As a speaker and presenter, I have to maintain a high level of energy and enthusiasm to get my message across and make an impact on those in the audience. I draw a big chunk of this energy from them. They're a huge reinforcement. And that energy goes two ways. When the audience meets my energy with theirs—wow—for the rest of the presentation, I'm constantly trying to pull that energy in, send it back, keep it flowing.

My energy can come from rapt attention to their applause and laughter. If they applaud and laugh and shake their heads, then I get that rush of energy that comes from appreciation and acknowledgement when my message resonates. Maybe that message took them to a deep place, or they appreciated my laughter, or my sense of humor came across.

On the other hand, there are signs when I'm not connecting at all—when the audience is restless, looking around the room, focusing on their phones, gazing longingly at the exits—signals that I need to change my approach quickly, course-correct now to keep them engaged.

And it's not just me. The audience members also feed off one another. For example, applause travels in waves through the room, and if the audience is scattered across multiple locations and different rooms, they can't see each other and feel each other, and then energy is lost. So, even when I do a virtual session, I try to have some kind of an audience in the room I'm in. Still, there's no substitute for having all the people who are listening to you, your talk, your message, in the same room. It's a shared experience. I can't do it by myself.

So while all the amazing technologies surrounding us help us to express our caring in ways that are quick and innovative, at the end of the day, we return to what has worked for more than 200,000 years. Proximity. Presence. Reaching out to others, with even the smallest gesture. Celebrating our humanity. It's contagious.

WILD
W😊MEN

Even after all this time, the sun never says to
the earth, "You owe me." Look what happens
with a love like that. It lights up the whole sky.

— Hafiz

In 2016, I flew with a team from Google to Kathmandu, Nepal, to explore if we could address the problem of human trafficking using technology. In India and Nepal, thousands of young girls from poor families are kidnapped and forced into prostitution each year, and Casey Allred, founder of Effect.org, is doing all he can to stop it. Every year, he brings in groups of people from two partnering companies—Google and Salesforce—to apply their talents and skills (such as coding, marketing, human resources, design) to developing new technology-based solutions during a hackathon. Volunteers then work with partnering nonprofits to develop and implement the solutions.

Part of the experience is immersing yourself in the culture, so we spent the first several days traveling by bus around the Kathmandu Valley, going to Nepalese villages, talking with local people, gaining a sense of life in poor rural areas, where the problem is the worst. By immersing ourselves in the culture and the causes of the problem, we developed a connection with and a greater understanding of the issues, and a deeper empathy and compassion for everyone involved.

Economics play a huge part. No family actually sends their daughter away thinking they're selling her to traffickers. The traffickers deceive these girls' families. Usually it's someone the family trusts, someone from the neighboring village who says there's a family that wants to take the girl in, give her a job as a maid or a waitress in Dubai or in the film industry in Mumbai. They tell the girl's parents this family will send their daughter to school, a luxury the parents themselves can't afford. In truth, these girls end up in brothels or working as entertainers in bars and restaurants. There's no school.

During our travels, I met three women involved in helping children—Sunita Danuwar, Menuka Thapa, and Nicole Thakuri-Wick—who, together, illustrate the resilience of the human spirit and the power of the collective to impact lives and change the world.

SUNITA DANUWAR

I met Sunita Danuwar in Kathmandu at one of Shakti Samuha's four shelter homes for girls rescued from sex trafficking. Sunita is a Nepalese activist and one of the loudest voices against sex trafficking on the international stage. She is also one of the founders and the acting president of Shakti Samuha, as well as a teacher and counselor.

Sunita was 14 years old when she was taken. After regaining consciousness in a brothel, she refused to have sex with the clients. The owner starved her, tortured her, and threatened her with death, but she wouldn't give in. Finally, more than three years later, the exasperated owner sold her to a brothel in Mumbai, where she again refused to have sex, until the owner ordered five men to rape her. After that, she was too tired to fight anymore, and she started seeing as many as 30 men per day (50 on holidays), seven days a week, anytime, day or night. Five months after that—four years after being sold into slavery—Sunita was rescued during a major raid of brothels in Mumbai. Nearly 500 women and girls (some as young as nine) were rescued from brothels that year.

After returning to Nepal, Sunita lived in a prison-like rehabilitation center. Fifteen women from that center, including Sunita Danuwar, determined that others shouldn't suffer as they had. They joined forces to form Shakti Samuha, with the purpose of spreading awareness about human trafficking and "organizing and empowering returning trafficking survivors by providing shelter, legal aid, vocational training and counseling." Sunita was still a teenager, and a traumatized young woman, when she co-founded the organization.

The literal English translation of Shakti Samuha is "Power Group." But the meaning goes deeper than that. In Hindi, *shakti* means energy, power, movement, change, nature, divine feminine energy. Every goddess in India has shakti. You don't mess with that kind of power. *Samuha* means group. Shakti Samuha, then, implies a collective force of divine feminine energy. Again, you don't mess with that.

Before arriving at the shelter, we'd been briefed about what to expect, what to say and not say. We were told these were very young girls who had been through something horrific. They were traumatized, and we needed to be careful about how we approached them, what we said. We were told (and later discovered) that some of the girls wouldn't make eye contact. On the other hand, some of them might be a little flirtatious with some of the guys in the group, because that was how they'd been trained to operate—that was how they'd survived. We were told to act normally while being respectful of what they'd been through and their individual process of healing.

The girls were told we were coming—this large group from the United States—and why. Normally the organization wouldn't have allowed a group like ours in. They're very guarded and fiercely protective of the girls' privacy. But they knew and trusted Casey, so we were allowed to visit.

When we first entered the center, I was struck by the energy, happiness, and empowerment of the girls. Some of them had only recently been rescued. And they were singing, dancing, and being playful like teenagers anywhere would be, filled with the innocence and joy I see in my goddaughter, Malaika, and my nieces, Devyani and Kalyani. With some exceptions, most of the girls were talking easily, giggling, and laughing.

They wanted to engage with us. Ask us questions. They were curious about the project we were working on. We weren't to talk to them about what they'd been through, so we asked them about their favorite colors, subjects in school, and questions that would help them dream— questions like "What do you want to do when you graduate?" Some wanted to be police officers or doctors. Some of the more mature girls wanted to go into law, politics, or activism to tackle the problem head-on. These girls were excited, filled with purpose, and very aware of their strength. There was such a sense of hope and possibility.

Once the girls grew comfortable with us, they started seeing us as a sort of extended family—fun people who'd come from outside and wanted to talk to them. We let our guard down, exhaled, grew more comfortable. Most of the girls spoke Hindi and watched Bollywood movies, and since I happened to know one of the latest Bollywood hits, I played it for them on my phone. They were so excited that I knew the song. They started singing and dancing to the music. And as we sang and danced with them, I was overcome by the sense of sweet, childlike innocence these girls had somehow managed to hold on to.

And I had to wonder: What in the human spirit allows someone to survive this type of trauma and demonstrate such resilience and joy? Sunita has a sense of purpose, a compassionate heart, and hope. She's a big believer in the power of hope. But what about these newly rescued girls? How had they kept their spirits intact?

I could see several ways.

First, at the shelters, there was love, protection, and both physical and psychological safety—all necessary for healing. Sunita and her co-founders had created an organization led completely by women who'd been in the same situation as these girls and had risen from that. There was a sense of "You and I have been through this."

Then, they were children, still very much in touch with their innocence, wonder, curiosity. Qualities that we, as adults, might have to work hard to connect with. They had tremendous human capacity to bounce back, to dig deep and find a sense of resilience that was extraordinary. I'm not saying everything was behind them and all was well. They'd have their demons—Sunita still has nightmares—but they were going forward, healing, reknitting, with so much courage and dignity.

Then there were the role models. Women who had instilled a sense of hope, empowerment, self-respect, and courage in the girls. For them, it was inspiration seeing what Sunita has done with her life. She's a firepower, out on the world stage, traveling around the globe, a strident voice raising awareness about this horrible crime, demanding action, fighting to put an end to it.

There was also a sense of deep respect for the human being in each of these girls, for their process, their dreams.

And, finally, there was a sense of purpose, everywhere. The girls are curious. They're studying, working, learning skills. They're being useful and productive.

I'm not saying this is the formula for everyone in every situation. But I witnessed it, and I believe it works. Shakti Samuha is helping the girls in their shelters work through the trauma of sex slavery, unearthing the beauty, joy, and sense of possibility that human beings are capable of. The big takeaway for me was simply this: that every human soul has this incredible capacity for happiness. We don't ever lose it. It's our fundamental quality. Despite the most difficult experiences, we can still come to a place of joy.

MENUKA THAPA

During that same trip, we visited Raksha Nepal, where I met Menuka Thapa. Menuka was the youngest of nine girls in a family on a quest for a boy. Her father died before her birth. Poverty forced her out of school even though she wanted to continue. She ended up in the street in the big city—Kathmandu. Social organizations wouldn't support her because she didn't qualify in any of their categories.

Left with no options, but blessed with a beautiful voice, she became a singer in a local restaurant. And that put her in touch with the community of women who worked in the hospitality industry, a community that was vulnerable and preyed upon. After personally witnessing the mistreatment and abuse of women in the restaurant, Menuka was motivated to work against it.

She went on to organize these entertainers, educate them about their rights, and give them the self-confidence to say no to compulsive prostitution and protect their sense of dignity. In 2004, while in her early 20s, she founded Raksha Nepal, which literally means "Protection Nepal," to give power and confidence to the women in that community and profession who were most vulnerable. The organization's main focus is to protect women and young girls working in massage parlors, dance bars, and cabin restaurants—a type of informal restaurant throughout Nepal—"from trafficking and sexual violence by enhancing their knowledge, awareness and socio-economic status."

One of the programs Menuka has created is to house and educate the children of these women so they're protected when their mothers are at work. While the mothers may not have a choice in the way they're earning a living, Menuka is determined to break the cycle so that their children—both daughters and sons—have options.

I saw these kids give a martial arts demonstration and was struck not just by their ju-jitsu chops, but also by the courage in their eyes, a quiet self-confidence. That is the extraordinary impact Menuka has had: she's taken these kids from the darkest situations, and she has helped them transform. She's demonstrated the triumph of the human spirit herself, and now she's sharing that spirit, uplifting others, lighting up lives.

NICOLE THAKURI-WICK

Finally, I met Nicole Thakuri-Wick, who grew up in Horgen, Switzerland. Her drive didn't stem from overcoming adversity, but from overwhelming love and compassion she wanted to share. In 1993, she was a student on a holiday trip to Nepal when she ran into some street kids in the streets of Kathmandu. She looked into their eyes and it changed her life forever. She called her mother and said, "Mom, can you send me some money?"

"Is this for your trip? Have you run out of money?"

"No, Mom. I'm renting a house in Nepal."

"A house in Nepal? What are you doing?"

"I'm moving in with six street kids I've adopted."

She was 23 years old.

I visited Nicole at her school, Nawa Asha Griha (NAG), or "Home of New Hopes." Her school is now home to 200 children for whom she provides food, clothing, shelter, and an education. In addition, she sends a school bus around daily to the local slums to collect 150 students who attend a school and also get books, meals, and uniforms. And if that isn't daunting enough, she supports another 300 local children who attend the local state school system.

I asked her what her mission was, and she said, "Gopi, I want to democratize education in this part of the world. Good-quality education is only affordable by and available to the elite. I want to make sure that everyone, including street children, have equal access to it."

All three of these women are dedicated to protecting and educating children, giving them the tools they need to build a strong sense of self, to live a life with opportunities, choices, freedom, and joy.

Although their economic backgrounds and life experiences are vastly different, these three have many things in common: They were young when they started. They had no financial resources. They had zero life experience in the work they embarked on. And they shared a conviction and fierce determination. They didn't know what failure was, so they didn't fear it. Most important, they were unstoppable. If they ran into a hurdle, which they did several times during their life's work, they simply figured a way around it.

What Sunita Danuwar, Menuka Thapa, and Nicole Thakuri-Wick are teaching all of us and the world is simply this—ordinary people with limited resources can have an extraordinary impact on the lives of others. These women have demonstrated the triumph of the human spirit, and the power of sharing that spirit so that others triumph with them.

A FINAL
JUMP FOR
JY

*The mystic chords of memory, stretching
from every battlefield and patriot grave to
every living heart and hearthstone all over
this broad land, will yet swell the chorus of the
Union, when again touched, as surely they will
be, by the better angels of our nature.*

— ABRAHAM LINCOLN, FINAL SENTENCE
OF HIS FIRST INAUGURAL ADDRESS

At the dawn of the Civil War in the United States, Abraham Lincoln gave his first inaugural address, his words primarily addressing the Southern states that had seceded from the Union. It was a terrible time, when everything the country had been founded on was being ripped to shreds. Lincoln invited William Seward, his rival for the presidency, to weigh in on his inaugural speech and had incorporated one of the suggestions as the final paragraph, with one tweak. In *A. Lincoln: A Biography*, Ronald C. White, Jr., writes of the six-word revision, which changed the meaning entirely: "Seward had written 'the guardian angel of the nation'—impersonal. But Lincoln invoked 'the better

179

angels of our nature'—deeply personal." Lincoln's words were a reminder that in times of upheaval, when things seem darkest, we need to pause and take a minute to focus on the pure human spirit in each one of us, the true good we can often lose sight of.

Today, the world seems to be twisting in on itself— natural disasters, political unrest, terrorism, unfathomable acts of violence, the rise of populism and nationalism, and tightening borders. It's easy to get depressed, upset, worried, to lose hope in life, this planet, and humanity in general. Yet I don't believe at this time in our history we've suddenly taken a nosedive. It's just that we're being exposed to so much more.

Seventy years ago, only small pieces of news may have trickled down to us in our local newspaper, and only if the paper had an international section that covered that part of the world. But now, with news feeds on our phones, tweets, Facebook posts, 24/7 news stations—the exposure is massive. With news, by definition, these events are going to make headlines. But even with all this violence and wreckage, there is good.

I went to Dallas recently to speak at a fund-raiser for Akshaya Patra, the world's largest NGO-run midday meal program. They serve wholesome school lunches to 1.6 million children in 13,839 schools across 12 states in India, for just 11 cents per child per day. Human resourcefulness and technical innovation allow them to perform the herculean task of cooking, portioning, and distributing so many meals each day. Yet a story such as this is rarely deemed newsworthy.

While we have to respond to the terrible news of disasters and suffering, there's also cause for much celebration— human beings are making tremendous progress forward, for themselves and for each other. Yet the massive flood of information coming at us makes it seem as though we're going backward—the trajectory of humans, cut off from our own humanity, soon to become a distant memory.

I recently came across an article—"Better and better"—in a 2016 copy of *The Economist* I'd stashed away. I'd held on to it for both the hopeful content of the entire article and the tone of the opening paragraph, which so hilariously reflects that of economists: "Humans are a gloomy species," the article begins, "since 71% of Britons think the world is getting worse; only 5% think it's improving. Asked whether global poverty has fallen by half, doubled, or remained the same, only 5% of Americans answered correctly that it's fallen by half. . . . People are predisposed to think that things are worse than they are, and they overestimate the likelihood of calamity. This is because they rely not on data, but on how we see this and recall an example. And bad things are more memorable. The media amplifies this distortion. Famines, earthquakes, and beheadings all make gripping headlines. '40 million planes landed last year' does not." The article goes on to say that "pessimism has political consequences." This is because we want to go back, to when we perceived times were better, instead of seeing progress and carrying it forward.

We need to move forward.

GETTING BETTER

In his 2011 book *Better Angels of Our Nature: Why Violence Has Declined*, Harvard psychologist Steven Pinker argues that things aren't getting worse, but better. Bill Gates wrote a review of the book in 2012, citing it as "one of the most inspiring books I've read—not just this year, but ever."

In 2017, Bill Gates tweeted, "[Pinker] shows how the world is getting better. Sounds crazy, but it's true. This is the most peaceful time in human history. If you think the world is getting better, you want to spread the progress to more people and places. It doesn't mean you ignore the serious problems we face. It just means you believe they can be solved."

So, at any point in time, you can always read articles, listen to lectures, and watch newscasts about all the problems associated with our healthcare system, transportation, urbanization, global warming, land use . . . Analysts and critics are often quick to comment about how things are rapidly deteriorating in our lives. And while I'm not disputing the fact that these are very real problems for which we need to find a solution, I maintain my sense of hope in how humanity as a whole is definitely improving the quality of life globally, and I agree with Bill Gates that maintaining this hope expands our sense of possibility and our ability to solve these problems, which, I believe, fuels more hope, more innovation, more solutions.

Swedish author and historian Johan Norberg also believes things are getting better. In his book *Progress: Ten Reasons to Look Forward to the Future*, he cites statistics showing we've made tremendous progress during the past 200 years.

- In 1820, 94 percent of humanity subsisted on less than $2 a day in today's dollars. In 1990, it dropped to 37 percent, and in 2015, 10 percent.

- In 1980, 24 percent of the world's population had modern sanitation, by 2016 it was up to 68 percent.

- The caste system in India is crumbling. In 1990, the proportion of upper-caste weddings with segregated seating was 75 percent. In 2008, that number fell to 13 percent.

- In 1987, only 58 percent of Americans approved of interracial dating. In 2012 that number rose to 86 percent (and 95 percent of 18–to–29-year-olds).

- Our ancestors in hunter-gatherer societies had a homicide rate that was approximately 500 times what it is in Europe today.

And the World Health Organization cites these statistics:

- Globally, the mortality rate for children under age five has decreased by 56 percent, from an estimated 93 deaths per 1,000 live births in 1990 to 41 deaths per 1,000 live births in 2016.

- From 2000 to 2015, the global population with access to at least basic drinking water services increased by 1.5 billion people.

So long-term, we're getting better. At the end of the day, no matter how bleak or dire things may seem, when we look at the progress we've made, we can feel a sense of hope, positivity, optimism, a cause to jump for joy, to celebrate, in our pursuit of happiness, the opportunities life presents, to explore our own talents and creativity and make it blossom. It leads to a fullness of life, and whatever it is, wherever you come from, in whatever state you're in, you push the boundaries, just for the sake of pushing them.

OPEN TO THE UNIVERSE

So how do you go about this blossoming? Where do you start?

First, ask yourself, *How much can I grow? How much can I bloom? What can I do with my gifts, talents, and capabilities?* Explore these questions for no other reason than to let yourself grow. Each of us is like a flower, here to experience a joyful existence, and like a flower, we want to grow, to bloom, to express that beauty and joy. This is the intrinsic nature of a flower. This is *dharma*, the law of the universe, and it's our dharma to allow it.

I sincerely believe this, and that's why we're all unique, individually created, to express ourselves as only we can, to offer the gift of our unique, joyous, happily bumbling selves. It's a stunning fact that an estimated 100 billion humans have walked this planet, lived and died, and as of this writing, 7.6 billion are still here, including you and me. We all have unique DNA, unique fingerprints, even identical twins. There hasn't been one repetition. How is it possible that in 100 billion, not one person has been replicated? You'd think that God would make a mistake at some point and stamp out a carbon copy, but he, she, or it hasn't done so. We're meant to be individual and different and unique and special. Whether we acknowledge it or not. So just allow your life to blossom and grow, just like a flower does, for its own sake.

Next, when you have an opportunity to provide acts of service and transform someone's life, do so. You don't have to be a Bill Gates with $45 billion in the Gates Foundation to do it. Simply by allowing yourself to open and expand, you uplift others. Think of a flower, when it's in full bloom, anyone who passes by can pause to take notice, smell, touch, feel, take a photograph. When I paused in my writing to gaze out the window a moment ago, I saw one early spring flower, just one, peeking out in the bed below. Whether I'm here or not, appreciating its beauty, the flower does its thing, standing there, turned toward the light of the sun. Just looking at that flower brings me joy. Human beings bring that same joy when expressing their joyous spirits. Think of little babies when they smile. It's a moment of joy for families.

Finally, when we come together to pool our energy, this is when we start transforming life for all in a positive way. We can turn things around. And we do want to turn things around. The U.K.'s National Council for Voluntary Organisations reported a 52 percent increase from 2010–2011 to 2014–2015 in volunteers aged 16 to 24, about one million more young volunteers. And look at the changes in traditional giving brought about by technology. The Internet and social media have opened the doors to organize and effect social change: driving online petitions through platforms like Change.org; tweeting and posting civic-minded videos; fund-raising for people in need through online platforms like GoFundMe and HopeMob.

Companies and organizations, universities, entire countries are focusing on happiness and well-being because they've come to realize the need to feel psychologically safe, energized, creative, excited. Happy. Why else would the Coca-Cola Company have created their Happiness Institute? Or three people from a company like Google publish three books on happiness? Why else would top universities such as Stanford, Yale, and Harvard offer courses on happiness? Or the United Arab Emirates create an entire ministry of happiness? And look at Bhutan, way ahead of the curve, which has measured the state of its citizens since the 1970s with its Gross National Happiness

Index, considered more important than the GDP? Why are happiness conferences, summits, festivals sprouting up all over? There's no denying it: people are thinking about happiness, talking about it, teaching it—all of which is cause to jump for joy. At the end of the day, despite all the bad news, there is more good news. We just need to stop, look deeper, pay attention to the good that's going on in the world. It's our opportunity and responsibility to taste the joy, feel it, experience it, create it. Add to it.

I want to close this book by asking you to wander off and ponder these questions: What will you do today to make yourself happy? What will you do today to make the people in your immediate life—it could be family, friends, colleagues—be a little happier? And then what will you do today to work with a larger circle of influence—your school, your workplace, your community—to add to this infinite pool of happiness?

Then, as Rilke wrote in *Letters to a Young Poet*, "Live the questions now." Why not? Take the leap. Make a mess of things. Have faith. Land softly.

ACKN☺WLEDGMENTS

I'm sitting in a Zurich cafe, dying to get out in the warm sunshine and bike toward the mountains and lakes that surround me. The lunchtime yoga class I just finished at the Sanapurna yoga studio (located on the very incongruous Militarstrasse) with some Zurich ladies (as is sometimes the case in a yoga studio, I was the only man) was lovely. I then quickly transitioned from downward dog on the yoga mat to upright man in the cafe chair I sit in now, because Kelly Malone and Anne Barthel are ready to strangle me if I don't turn this in. One of the drawbacks of technology is that my editors can track me down within one square meter anywhere in the world to remind me of the impending deadlines that weigh heavily on my conscience. I can no longer plead distance and remoteness. Or hide behind inaccessibility and infallibility.

But then writing the acknowledgments for *The Happy Human* is an easy job. I get to think of all the people who make me happy and who made this book possible, which in turn makes me happy.

Front and center are my parents, who gave me life. And who gave me happiness from the day I was born. My father, who witnessed the birth of this book and was very proud of it, passed away less than a year before it shipped. I know he's smiling and happy.

Thank you, Amma and Achan. This work is dedicated to both of you.

My spiritual teachers, Rama Devi, Tara Devi, and Amma, who taught me that I could be responsible for my happiness by connecting to my inner-net. That happiness has less to do with changing my externalities and more to do with changing my consciousness. And the only lasting happiness is internally generated.

Kelly Malone, my angel-in-writing. She coaxed and cajoled the book out of me over three years. She project-managed me remotely as I darted in and out of mysterious airports and secret hotels. And she brilliantly helped shape its narrative. Most important, when my insecurities ran high, she reassured me it was a good book. And she always responded with patience, grace, and a sense of humor. God knows you need that in abundance when you have me as the author. Her grasp of infinitives, gerunds, predicates, and antecedents is legendary. What the heck are those anyway? Does anyone else know or care?

I highly recommend her if you're thinking of a book in the future and are devoid of talent, like me.

Anne Barthel, my editor at Hay House, who took 50,000 words in a Word file and manifested the book that is in your hands now. It's a mystery and marvel to me. The black box process. We craft an e-mail, attach manuscript file, and press Send. Then Anne and her team go to work shaping the book. Lasering typos and dangling modifiers. Adding color and cover. Juggling dates and deadlines, design and production schedules. Always showing grace under pressure and providing wise counsel. Until a few months later, they ship the beautiful, fully produced, shiny new product that is in your hands, complete with that olfactory, evanescent specialty—the new product smell.

Stephanie Tade, my agent, always calm and unruffled. It must have something to do with years of dealing with rogue authors like me and her dedicated Buddhist meditation practice. She knows it will get done. She also knows the right time to reach out, give our writing-process prayer wheel one more spin, and grease it with a little yak butter, while we peer into the darkness, mumbling writer incantations and hoping for some brilliant literary enlightenment.

Leah Foley, our transcriber, who toils away in rainy Dublin as she downs the Irish national water. She can make sense of my loquacious prattle in a Malayalee-English accent, and by the time the earth has spun around, ship us back something that's finally beginning to make sense to Kelly and me. And in a tamer rendition of her Irish brogue, "It's bloody brilliant."

Reid Tracy, CEO of Hay House, who six years ago famously said in his soft accent, "I think we should do a deal." And thus unleashed another starving author into the literary madhouse.

My siblings, Ravi, Kala, and Sathi. Their spouses, Manju, Sudhakaran, and Manoharan. And my nieces and nephew—Shalini, Devi, Devyani, Kalyani, and Suneil. Ours is a tight-knit family, always a circle of happiness and psychological safety even under difficult life circumstances.

Thank you to Stuart Newton, or "Captain Happy" as his playa name goes, my dear friend and mentor. He and his lovely wife, Darcie, have been my Burning Man housemates for years. It was Stuart's famous phrase one early morning—"Happy Human is higher than any other title you can attain"—that set me down the speeding path toward this book. It was manifest destiny.

Henry Miller, my first speech coach, and more recently, Claudette O'Neil and Paulette Jacome, along with Melissa Goldman. Between them they've taught me to speak and speak well, and four times carried me on their shoulders to the semifinals of Toastmaster's International World Championship of Public Speaking. As I write this, we're preparing for this year's world championship in August 2018. It's their skills that will help me speak about this book once it launches. Claudette is also a school teacher. Appropriately, she stayed up one night to read the whole early version of the book in one sitting (something even I couldn't do), recording all suggested changes in a neat tabular document. Exactly as the world's greatest teachers do.

Ananta Govinda, my music producer, who helped get our second album, *Kirtan Lounge: Precious Jewels*, into consideration for the 2018 Grammy awards, which made all members of our music collective very happy. And managed the digital and social branding and identity of this book.

Special thanks to Jewel and her management team Marc Oswald and Steve Schweidel. I knew Jewel simply as the beautiful singer-songwriter from Alaska who had the impossible life trajectory of living in her car in San Diego, to singing in coffee shops for bagels, to winding up with four Grammy nominations and more than 30 million albums sold. Before we met, I had obsessively listened to *Pieces of You* and tried to answer "Who will save my soul?" and "Who was meant for me?" as well as much of her subsequent lyrical masterpieces. No Indian astrologer had ever predicted our paths would cross, but, there we were, all together at the dinner table at the Wisdom 2.0 conference in San Francisco in 2017, where she and I were fellow speakers.

Jewel was charming and gave me a signed copy of her book *Never Broken: Songs Are Only Half the Story*. She describes her life's message to the world—making happiness a habit—on her website (www.jewelneverbroken.com), which she calls "an emotional fitness destination that gives you the tools you need to create change in your life."

Thank you, Marc and Steve, for submitting our album for Grammy consideration in five categories, including Best World Music album. Suddenly a door had opened, and we were happily and blindly hurtling down a path we knew nothing about. Ready to live life fully. Ready to fail. I'm so grateful to all of you for believing in me.

Tal Ben-Shahar, whose course on happiness was the most popular at Harvard ever, for graciously agreeing to write the foreword. Thank you for adding so much legitimacy to the book. I am humbled.

Malaika, my little princess and goddaughter whom I adore, I love to dote on you and spoil you because that makes me happy. Your spirited nature reminds me that we are all indeed alive and human.

Anna, or RD, as our secret handshake would have it, a polymath who's mastered two complex legal systems in two languages, understands Vedic philosophy, and sings with a divine voice, between yoga and kirtan, magic moments from Rovinj, Croatia, to Paradise Island, Bahamas, to Kuttanad, Kerala, as well as regular reliable messages, you keep me grounded and walking my path to happiness. Thank you for inspiring me to lead a healthier life and raise my consciousness, and for creating much joy in my life.

Alan Eagle, coauthor of *How Google Works*, for teaching me many things on my own journey. And for giving me the freedom and empowerment to lead my highest professional life.

Jonathan Rosenberg, also the coauthor of *How Google Works* and a longtime mentor at Google, for sharing my passion for, and pushing the boundaries of my skills in, persuasive storytelling.

Margo Georgiadis, one of my most inspiring leaders at Google, you taught me much about how to show up in life, and that's why one of your anecdotes is in this book.

Philipp Schindler, Chief Business Officer at Google, who leads intensely from the front and yet, by setting a personal example to find balance, challenges us to do the same, reminding us that we can only be truly happy if we're at a peak state of both aspects of our lives.

Several leaders at Google who are inspiring as well as extremely down-to-earth and human. The *human* part of *The Happy Human* was often derived from simply watching them in action, and their stories and wisdom found their way into the book—Sundar Pichai, Susan Wojcicki, Lorraine

Twohill, Allan Thygesen, Jim Lecenski, Eileen Naughton, Patrick Pichette, Laszlo Boch, Tara Levy, and Paul Ferrand.

Silvia Cabrera, Haley Schulz, and Joyce Peng, who at various points in the book's creation managed my speaking and writing schedules. Thank you, ladies, for keeping my life and schedule sane and making sure that I showed up in whichever city in the world I was supposed to show up on the right day and time, and handling so much more.

To conclude, as humans, our happiness is also the result of cocreation with others—our happiness tribe. The people we can choose to surround us with who can always make us laugh, whose mere presence, smile, touch makes us a little bit happier. We all need our tribe to survive, to be happy. This is a partial member list of my happiness tribe—Tree, Meena, Suku, TT, Vas, Manpreet, Naseem, Sabari, Babu, Binod, Alka, Atul, Malini, and Neha.

The Wharton tribe: Maureen, Wilf, Heidi, Ben, David, Coop, Heather, Gwyn, Laura, Ted, Alissa, Linda, Julie, Melissa, Mei, Mark, and Kate.

The IIMC tribe: Shyam, Maya, John, Paddy, Deven, Shanks, Naren, Hash, and Lala.

The NIIT tribe: Mali, Mag, Kumar, DK, Jaap, Sandy, and GI.

The Burner tribe: Pele, Bear, Katy, Evan, Charlotte, Hannah, Brad, Kali Das, Tony, and Ximena.

The Conscious community: Sara, Jahnavi, Vijay, Nath, Kika, Adrienne, Matt, and Arnaud.

You Make Me Happy club: Whitney, Sierra, Amandine, Sara, Katy, Sonia, and Susannah.

An attitude of gratitude is one of the greatest pathways to happiness. Recognizing your interdependency and being willing to surrender to the vulnerability is another. I am grateful to all of you.

AB😊UT THE AUTHOR

Gopi Kallayil is Chief Brand Evangelist, Brand Marketing at Google; the founder of the yoga program for Googlers, called Yoglers; and the self-proclaimed "Happy Human," a title his business card bears above his name. Having become a yoga teacher by studying at the Sivananda Ashram Neyyar Dam, Kerala, India, Gopi is an avid yoga practitioner. He is also a triathlete, global traveler, and Burning Man devotee. He often tells people he feels lucky to have won the ovarian lottery, meaning he feels incredibly blessed to have been born into a culture where practicing meditation and mindfulness have been a part of people's daily lives for hundreds of years, an integral part of the culture and spiritual traditions of that land. He carries that influence into all that he does.

Gopi earned his bachelor's degree in electronics engineering from the National Institute of Technology in India. He received two master's degrees in business administration, one from the Indian Institute of Management and one from The Wharton School of Business at the University of Pennsylvania. Gopi has delivered more than 100 talks on topics such as meditation, mindfulness in business practices, the dharma of business, corporate culture, and yoga. He has spoken at TEDx, the World Happiness Summit, Yoga Journal LIVE!, and Wisdom 2.0. Gopi holds a guest faculty position teaching brand marketing at the Stanford University Graduate School of Business and serves on the board of the Desmond Tutu Peace Foundation. He's the author of *The Internet to the Inner-Net* and has released two music albums (Kirtan Lounge). Website: www.kallayil.com

Hay House Titles of Related Interest

YOU CAN HEAL YOUR LIFE, the movie,
starring Louise Hay & Friends
(available as a 1-DVD program, an expanded
2-DVD set, and an online streaming video)
Learn more at www.hayhouse.com/louise-movie

THE SHIFT, the movie,
starring Dr. Wayne W. Dyer
(available as a 1-DVD program, an expanded
2-DVD set, and an online streaming video)
Learn more at www.hayhouse.com/the-shift-movie

*EVERYTHING IS HERE TO HELP YOU: A Loving Guide
to Your Soul's Evolution,* by Matt Kahn

*A FIELD GUIDE TO HAPPINESS: What I Learned in Bhutan
about Living, Loving, and Waking Up,* by Linda Leaming

*MORE BEAUTIFUL THAN BEFORE:
How Suffering Transforms Us,* by Steve Leder

*WAKING UP IN PARIS: Overcoming Darkness
in the City of Light,* by Sonia Choquette

All of the above are available at your local bookstore,
or may be ordered by contacting Hay House (see next page).

We hope you enjoyed this Hay House book. If you'd like to receive our online catalog featuring additional information on Hay House books and products, or if you'd like to find out more about the Hay Foundation, please contact:

Hay House, Inc., P.O. Box 5100, Carlsbad, CA 92018-5100
(760) 431-7695 or (800) 654-5126
(760) 431-6948 (fax) or (800) 650-5115 (fax)
www.hayhouse.com® • www.hayfoundation.org

Published in Australia by: Hay House Australia Pty. Ltd.,
18/36 Ralph St., Alexandria NSW 2015
Phone: 612-9669-4299 • *Fax:* 612-9669-4144
www.hayhouse.com.au

Published in the United Kingdom by: Hay House UK, Ltd.,
The Sixth Floor, Watson House, 54 Baker Street, London W1U 7BU
Phone: +44 (0)20 3927 7290 • *Fax:* +44 (0)20 3927 7291
www.hayhouse.co.uk

Published in India by: Hay House Publishers India,
Muskaan Complex, Plot No. 3, B-2, Vasant Kunj, New Delhi 110 070
Phone: 91-11-4176-1620 • *Fax:* 91-11-4176-1630
www.hayhouse.co.in

Access New Knowledge.
Anytime. Anywhere.

Learn and evolve at your own pace
with the world's leading experts.

www.hayhouseU.com

Printed in the United States
By Bookmasters